Great Hauntings

Great Hauntings

The world's most fascinating and best-documented phantoms

Editor: Peter Brookesmith

Orbis Publishing · London

Acknowledgments

Photographs were supplied by Anglia TV, BBC Hulton Picture Library, John Beedle, Boston Athenaeum Library, Bridgeman Art Library, British Tourist Authority, Richard Burgess, Clyde Surveys, Country Life, J Cutten, Arnold Desser, Robert Estall, Mary Evans Picture Library, J Forman, Robert H Gibbons, Colin Godman, Jim Hancock, Hodder and Stoughton, Toby Hogarth, Mike Hooks, Robert Hunt Library, Institut fur Grenzgebiete der Psychologie und Psychohygiene, Maurice Johannesburg, Keystone, Mansell Collection, Medical Illustrations Service, Jeannie Morison, National Portrait Gallery London, National Portrait Gallery Scotland, Peter Newark's Western Americana, Picturepoint, Psychic News, Mike Reynolds, Royal Commission on Ancient and Historical Monuments of Scotland, J Rundle, Ronald Sheridan, Spectrum Colour Library, J Strang, Syndication International, DC Thomson, John Topham Library, UPI, Peter Underwood, J Whitelaw.

Consultants to The Unexplained
Professor A.J. Ellinson
Dr J. Allen Hynek
Brian Inglis
Colin Wilson
Editorial Director
Brian Innes
Editor
Peter Brookesmith
Deputy Editor
Lynn Picknett
Executive Editor
Lesley Riley
Sub Editors
Mitzi Bales
Chris Cooper
Jenny Dawson
Hildi Hawkins

Picture Researchers
Anne Horton
Paul Snelgrove
Frances Vargo
Editorial Manager
Clare Byatt
Art Editor
Stephen Westcott
Designer
Richard Burgess
Art Buyer
Jean Morley
Production Co-ordinator
Nicky Bowden
Volume Editors
Lorrie Mack
Eric Harwood
Francis Ritter

First published in the United Kingdom by Orbis Publishing Limited, London

Marketed in the United States of America by Jilli Jay Enterprises Inc., Garnerville, New York 10923, U.S.A.

Material in this publication previously appeared in the weekly partwork *The Unexplained*, © 1980–83

Printed and bound in Italy by Arnoldo Mondadori, Verona

Contents

Introduction

ON THE VERY LAST DAY of the Second World War in Europe, when the shooting and bombing and carnage had ceased, my uncle Edward, serving in the Coldstream Guards, was killed in a minor railway accident near Berlin. He had survived almost five years of bloodshed and unparalleled violence and yet there he was at the end, dead not through human malice but the malfunction of machinery.

His mother, my grandmother, was very old and living in Yorkshire. She was senile and rarely left her fireside chair, but on that particular morning she grasped the head of her walking stick and rose to her feet when my mother entered.

'Teddy is dead,' she said. 'I've just seen him in his altar boy clothes.'

As far as my mother could make out, the vision had been that of her brother when he was about ten years old, a time when he had served at Mass wearing his white cotta and red cassock. When he died he was in his early twenties, wearing his khaki 'walking-out' dress uniform, complete with Sam Browne belt. Two days later a War Office telegram confirmed the news that the accident had happened at the time my grandmother had seen the 'ghost' of her son.

Such stories are commonplace in the annals of psychical research and even have a name: 'crisis apparitions.' But are they 'ghosts' in the sense of revenant spirits? The general theory is that at the emotionally supercharged moment of death the spirit projects itself onto the consciousness of those nearest to it in life; but this theory, as we shall see on later pages, has a drawback. On many occasions, the 'vision' seen has been that of a live person, going through a moment of intense happiness, relief, or fear. Many well attested wartime 'crisis apparitions' later turned out to have occurred at a moment when the subject was wounded or in grave danger, even though he or she eventually survived.

Indeed, the majority of true life 'ghosts' seem to have relevance not to the dead but to the living. Most poltergeist phenomena appear to centre around pre-pubescent or disturbed persons, though the celebrated 18th century Cock Lane ghost recalled in this book may be said to fit into the 'returned spirit' category of hauntings. Other hauntings could well be the result of wishful thinking, of people wanting to believe in a life beyond our own.

I am convinced that the famous haunting at Borley Rectory, Suffolk, was one of these examples. A 19th century incumbent liked to tell his daughters and parishoners that his house and garden were haunted; later his daughters fostered the rumour. Still later, the neurotic wife of another rector appears to have 'staged' incidents at the house, as a result of which the popular press became interested and asked the late Harry Price, who had made his name as a ghost hunter, to investigate. There seems little doubt today that Price was not a man of great integrity when it came to solid facts; his books and articles on the subject of Borley promoted the ugly building as 'the most haunted house in England', yet a closely analysed examination of the events he described, produced by three prominent members of the Society for Psychical Research in the 1950s, showed little evidence of anything but sheer chicanery on Price's part.

Nevertheless the site of Borley Rectory is still the object of pilgrimages by amateur ghost hunters from all over the world. Though the house itself burned down some years before Price's death in 1948, reports still surface of phantom nuns walking in what was once the garden, and a ghostly carriage and horses thundering down the hill towards the nearby town of Long Melford. In the 1970's, attention shifted to the parish church itself, and reliable investigators – including a team from the BBC – have recorded what appear to be inexplicable noises: grunts, heavy sighs, the sound of metallic objects being thrown down the aisle, and ponderous footsteps in the ancient church. Apparently, all precautions were taken to preclude any natural or fraudulent effects finding their way onto the tapes, and the results are impressive. But in the subjective, empirical world of paranormal theory, who can say exactly what the cause was? Experiments seem to show that the mind can have power over matter; perhaps the years of obsession with Borley as a haunted spot have finally impinged themselves onto it, producing 'genuine' as opposed to Harry Price's 'fake' phenomena.

The integrity of witnesses and researchers is, of course, vital in any attempt to assimilate the paranormal into a universal scheme of things. Many a good chilling ghost story must have its origin in, say, a drunken farmer stumbling home from the village pub, mistaking a sheep for an ethereal presence in the darkness, retailing his experience and laying the foundations of a piece of folk lore.

Some years ago, while writing on the supernatural for a magazine named *Man, Myth and Magic* I found so many examples of such unreliable stories that I decided to 'plant' one of my own. As outlined on page 74 of the present book, I invented the 'Phantom Vicar of Ratcliffe Dock,' and wrote about my creation in the magazine.

I determined, however, that if any researcher approached me for information on the subject, I would confess to my fakery; only one journalist, Bill Grundy who was then with Thames Television and has always been a paragon of professionalism, did so. When I eventually 'confessed' in the *Sunday Times* and later on BBC-2's *A leap in the dark* series, there was an outcry from the motley crew of popular ghost hunters who carry on the traditions of Harry Price. One claimed that the 'phantom vicar' had been a real ghost, who had somehow influenced me into making him 'come true.' Another, who had inherited Price's seat as secretary of a rather whimsical ghost club, described me in his autobiography as 'unscrupulous'; the truth is that both persons had

Tens of thousands of people were burned at the stake in Europe during the late medieval period. Some of these unfortunates had committed no greater sin than believing they had heard or seen a spirit

been caught out by a deliberate fraud which they made no effort to detect.

Oddly enough, despite newspaper and television articles relating what I had done, the 'phantom vicar' continues to thrive, and I was assured by the landlord of a local pub that my story of the *fake* had been an invention; the ghostly vicar himself had been well known in the area for years.

The whole world of the paranormal lends itself to fraud, both deliberate and accidental, but there are many cases on record which are not easily dismissed. The case of Frendraught House in Aberdeenshire, told on page 56, is a case in point. Here we have an historical record of events which happened in 1630, and a long tradition of sightings. Mrs Yvonne Morison, the owner's wife, is a person of the utmost integrity and common sense, who had nothing to lose or gain by claiming to have heard ghostly footsteps in the house; nor had her guests – who fled Frendraught in terror after hearing bumps and crashes in the night. Again in Scotland, Glamis Castle, the childhood home of the Queen Mother, has a centuries old reputation for being inhabited by a creature or creatures not of this world, and far from being glamorous the stories have been a source of annoyance and even trepidation to successive Earls of Strathmore.

Most students of the paranormal would put down the haunting of places like Frendraught and Glamis to the 'psychic recording' catalogue of such events (violence or tumultuous emotion which impregnates the site on which it has occurred by a sort of preternatural osmosis), a chronic form of the 'crisis apparitions' mentioned earlier. The Dower House at Killakee in Ireland has a history of such violence ranging from the early eighteenth century, when it was the haunt of 'Hellfire Club' rakes, to the twentieth century, when IRA gunmen shot each other to death there. Almost everyone has experienced a building which exudes a feeling of tranquility, of having been loved; perhaps extremes of anger and hatred leave behind a stronger residue.

The battlefield hauntings recalled by Joan Forman seem to reflect this, particularly in the impressive case of Edgehill, when that English Civil War battle was re-enacted on at least two occasions in front of witnesses who had been present at the original fight, and who recognised in the midst of the ghostly melée not only men who had died, but some who were still very much alive. In the case of Edgehill there appears to be no case of revenant spirits; more of an 'action replay' on some supernatural three-dimensional television screen.

Once having become part of legend, a ghost story is notoriously difficult to lay; classic cases in point are the 'screaming skull' legends retold here. In the case of 'Owd Nance' of Burton Agnes Hall, Yorkshire, we have an historic record to work on, the head of a former occupant having been kept in the hall at his sentimental if gruesome last request. But the screaming skull of Bettiscombe in Dorset, the basis for a ghostly tale by that master of spirit fiction Montague Rhodes James, is of much greater antiquity. Despite legends that the skull is that of a Negro slave, or of a woman mysteriously kept locked up in the house many years ago, fairly recent research seems to show that it is the cranium of a prehistoric woman: perhaps a 'foundation sacrifice' laid down to protect the original building on the site whose memory has been kept alive by that tenuous but enduring process 'folk tradition.'

What, however, are we to make of 'soulless ghosts' – the ships, coaches, and latterly aeroplanes and at least one red London bus? We might, to paraphrase one writer, be prepared to believe in the spirits of people and animals, but what of phantom shoes, shirts, and hats – for few ghosts ever seem to appear naked. Do modesty and decorum play a part in the afterlife?

Despite years of writing and broadcasting on the subject of apparitions, the 'family ghost' of my uncle is the nearest I have ever consciously come to experiencing one. I say consciously, because 'real life' spooks, as opposed to those of fiction, invariably appear as solid, lifelike figures; only when they suddenly walk through a wall or disappear are their observers filled with alarm and sometimes despondency. Undoubtedly the hundreds of people who have such psychic experiences cannot all be frauds, liars, or lunatics; *something* happens – but what?

The truth is that ghosts resolutely avoid being tested under laboratory conditions, thus putting them beyond the pale as far as orthodox science is concerned. They obey no one set of rules, and cannot be any more than loosely catagorised. In short they are a chilling but fascinating enigma: long may they remain so!

FRANK SMYTH

Borley: a haunting tale

Was Borley Rectory really 'the most haunted house in England' – or was its fame built on a great publicity stunt by ghost hunter Harry Price? Indeed, was Price a headline-seeking fraud? FRANK SMYTH **investigates**

BORLEY PARISH CHURCH stands on a hillside overlooking the valley of the river Stour, which marks the boundary between the counties of Essex and Suffolk in England. Borley can hardly even be called a village: the hundred or so inhabitants of this Essex parish, mainly agricultural workers and weekend cottagers, do their shopping and socialising in Long Melford or Sudbury, the two nearest small towns on the Suffolk side; for more important business they travel from Borley Green to Bury St Edmunds, about 25 miles (40 kilometres) away.

But in 1940 the publication of a book entitled *The most haunted house in England* made the community world famous, and in 1946 a further volume, *The end of Borley Rectory*, set the seal on its fame. Both were written by the flamboyant ghost hunter Harry Price, who made psychical research headlines in his day. The two books claimed that Borley Rectory, a gloomy Victorian house that had burned down in 1939, was the centre of remarkably varied paranormal phenomena. These included a phantom coach, a headless monk, a ghostly nun who may or may not have been the monk's lover, the spirit of a former vicar, eerie lights, water that turned into ink, mysterious bells, and a multifarious cascade of things that went bump in the night.

'One of the events of the year 1940' was how the first book was described by *Time and Tide* in its glowing review, while the *Church Times* said that it would 'remain among the most remarkable contributions ever made to the study of the paranormal'. Price, who professed to have devoted 10 years to his study of Borley's ghosts, continued to lecture, broadcast and write on the subject until his death on 29 March 1948. An obituary in *The Times* the following day summed him up as a psychical researcher with 'a singularly honest and clear mind on a subject that by its very nature lends itself to all manner of trickery and chicanery'.

Not everyone who knew or worked with Price agreed with this glowing testimonial, however. Some months after his death, and with the danger of libel safely out of the way, an article by Charles Sutton of the *Daily Mail* appeared in the *Inky way annual*, a World's Press News publication. Writing of a visit he had paid to Borley in 1929, in the

Borley Church, whose vicars lived in the reputedly haunted Borley Rectory not far away. Harry Price, ghost hunter, psychical researcher and author, put the parish of Borley 'on the map' when he wrote a book about the rectory hauntings in 1940

middle of Price's first investigation with another colleague, Sutton said that he had discovered what might be fraud on Price's part. After a large pebble had hit Sutton on the head, he found that Price had 'bricks and pebbles' in his pockets.

On a more careful investigation, two members of the Society for Psychical Research (SPR) – Lord Charles Hope and Major the Hon. Henry Douglas-Home – had had serious doubts about 'phenomena' they had witnessed at the rectory in the late 1920s. Both of them filed testimony with the SPR stating that they had grave suspicions. Douglas-Home went as far as to accuse Price of having a 'complete disregard for the truth in this matter'. He told how, on one occasion, he was accompanying Price around the rectory in the darkness when they heard a rustling that reminded him of cellophane being crumpled. Later, he sneaked a look into Price's suitcase and found a roll of cellophane with a torn edge.

It was as a result of this testimony that the Council of the SPR invited three of their members, Dr Eric J. Dingwall, Mrs K. M. Goldney and Mr Trevor H. Hall, to undertake a new survey of the evidence. The three were given access to Price's private papers and correspondence by his literary executor, Dr Paul Tabori. They also had access to documents in the Harry Price Collection, which Price had placed on permanent loan to the University of London in 1938 and bequeathed to that institution on his death. This survey took five years to prepare and was published in 1956 under the title *The haunting of Borley rectory*.

The reviews of this book were as enthusiastic as those of Price's two volumes in the 1940s, although for diametrically different reasons. The *Sunday Times* said that the Borley legend had been demolished 'with clinical thoroughness and aseptic objectivity', while Professor A.G.N. Flew in the *Spectator* commented that the 'shattering and fascinating document' had proved that Borley had been 'a house of cards built by the late Harry Price out of little more than a pack of lies'.

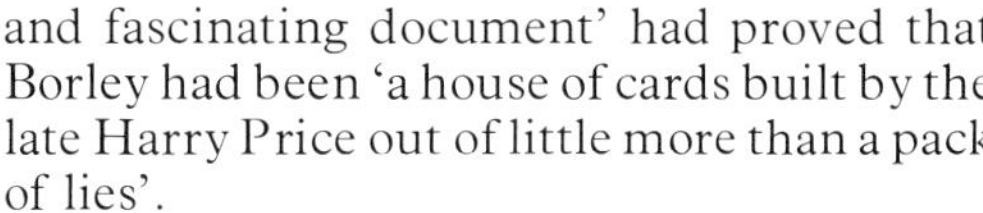

Price in action: on the radio direct from a haunted house in Meopham, Kent, in 1936 (above) and on a much-publicised trip to Germany with C.E.M. Joad to re-create a magical scene on the Brocken in the Harz mountains in 1932 (below)

There, perhaps, the matter should have rested, but due to a combination of factors it did not. The principal reason may have been that Borley had made sensational copy for the world's popular newspapers for over a quarter of a century, and even the most objective of reporters dislikes seeing a good source dry up. Newspapers and television programmes glossed over the painstaking evidence of Dingwall, Goldney and Hall, one referring to them as 'the scoffers who accused Harry Price, the greatest of ghost seekers, of rigging the whole legend'. And once more, the events described by Price were said to be 'puzzling, frightening, and inexplicable'. Peter Underwood, the president of the Ghost Club, and the late Dr Tabori returned to Price's defence in 1973 with a book entitled *The ghosts of Borley: annals of the haunted rectory*. They dedicated it to 'the memory of Harry Price, the man who put Borley on the map'.

In his book *The occult*, published in 1971, Colin Wilson made a fair and scrupulously unbiased summing up of the evidence for and against the Borley case. His conclusion was that 'a hundred other similar cases could be extracted [from SPR records]. . . . Unless someone can produce a book proving that Price was a pathological liar with a craving for publicity, it is necessary to suspend judgement.'

And, indeed, in 1978 SPR investigator Trevor H. Hall set out to prove Price 'a pathological liar with a craving for publicity'. The title of his book, *Search for Harry Price*, was a pun based on Price's own autobiography *Search for truth* (1942).

Had it been less carefully documented, Hall's book could have been fairly described as a piece of muckraking. He revealed, for instance, that Price's father was a London grocer who had seduced and married Price's mother when she was 14 and he was over 40. Price himself, in his autobiography, had claimed to be the son of a wealthy paper manufacturer who came of 'an old Shropshire family'.

Price stated that his childhood had been spent between the London stockbroker suburb of Brockley and the family's country home in an unnamed part of Shropshire. He said that he usually 'broke his journey' there on the way to and from school, implying that he was educated at a boarding school in the country. Hall's researches clearly showed the family home to have been in New Cross, not far from, but far less salubrious than, Brockley. Price, said Hall, attended a local secondary school, Haberdasher's Aske's Hatcham Boys' School, a perfectly respectable lower middle class establishment, but not a public boarding school. The only family connection

Above: Peter Underwood, the president of the Ghost Club, who came down on the side of Price in the controversy over the latter's integrity

Below: the ruins of Borley Rectory four years after it was completely destroyed by a mysterious fire. This did not end the speculation over its haunting

with Shropshire was that Price's grandfather had once been landlord of the Bull's Head at Rodington.

According to Price, he had held a directorship in his father's paper manufacturing company after leaving school, spending the 10 years between the end of his schooldays and his marriage in 1908 pleasantly as an amateur coin collector and archaeologist. In fact, according to Hall, Price earned his living in New Cross in a variety of odd ways. He took photographs of local shopfronts for advertising purposes; hired out his portable gramophone and records for dances, parties and other functions; performed conjuring tricks at concerts – a skill that he was later accused of using during his Borley investigation – and peddled glue, paste and a cure for footrot in sheep from door to door in the Kent countryside. Price had an indubitable flair for writing, as the impressive sales of his books – some 17 in all – testify.

In 1902 Price wrote an article for his old school magazine, *The Askean*, about the excavation of a Roman villa in Greenwich Park, quoting as his source a book written by the director of the project. By 1942, in *Search for truth*, he was claiming that he had actually helped to excavate the site. He also contributed a series of articles to the *Kentish Mercury* on coins and tokens of the county, following this up with another series for Shropshire's *Wellington Journal* on 'Shropshire tokens and mints'.

Hall asked the Reverend Charles Ellison, Archdeacon of Leeds and a leading authority

Left: Haberdasher's Aske's Hatcham Boys School, where Price had his education, as it looks today. According to Price's detractor, Trevor H. Hall, Price hinted in his autobiography that he had attended a public school

Below: the Harry Price Library in the Senate House at London University. Price bequeathed to the university his outstanding collection of thousands of books on magic and the occult – which Hall characterises as Price's 'most useful achievement'. Price also tried to get the university to establish a psychical research department, but failed. Some say that the institution was scared off by his flamboyant approach to scientific investigation

on numismatics, to examine Price's writings on coins. The archdeacon found them to be straight plagiarisms from two obscure works on the subject. 'It is unsafe to rely on any statement made by Harry Price which lacks independent confirmation,' he concluded.

Hall reported that Price's financial independence came from his marriage to Constance Knight, who inherited a comfortable fortune from her father. It was her means, and not family wealth as claimed, that gave him the leisure to put his days of door-to-door peddling behind him and embark on his career as psychical researcher and book collector. The assembling of a library of occult and magical books running into several thousand volumes was, said Hall, 'Price's most useful achievement during his life'.

Even the library seemed to offer opportunities for chicanery, however. In the collection Hall found several valuable books clearly marked with the imprint of the SPR. Price had catalogued them as his own, even attaching his own book plate.

Price's book plates were a source of interest and amusement for Hall, as well as another example of Price's covertness. Price used two crested plates. One featured a lion rampant and proved on investigation to be the family crest of Sir Charles Rugge-Price of Richmond, with whom Harry Price had no connection. The other, bearing a crest and coat of arms, carried the name 'Robert Ditcher-Price' and the address 'Norton Manor, Radnor'. Hall's investigations revealed that the crest and arms were those of Parr of Parr, Lancashire, and that Norton Manor belonged to Sir Robert Green-Price, Baronet, whose family had lived there since the 17th century. A letter from Lady Jean Green-Price unequivocally stated that she had never heard of Robert Ditcher-Price and that she was 'quite certain that he never resided at Norton Manor'.

In his first book on Borley Rectory in 1940 Price used a version of the 'nun's tale' supplied by the Glanville family – father Sydney, son Roger and daughter Helen. While holding a seance with a planchette at their home, Helen Glanville elicited the information that a nun had indeed been murdered at Borley and that she was a Frenchwoman called Marie Lairre. On the subject of this and subsequent seances he held, Sydney Glanville was almost apologetic to SPR researchers Dingwall, Goldney and Hall, admitting that suggestion had played a part: all three Glanvilles had studied the history of the Borley hauntings.

After the story of the French nun's ghost appeared in *The most haunted house in England*, Price received an elaborate theory from Dr W. J. Phythian-Adams, Canon of Carlisle, to the effect that Marie Lairre had been induced to leave her convent and marry one of the local landowners. She had been strangled by her husband and buried in a

Three of Harry Price's book plates. The one on the far right, bearing the name of 'Robert Ditcher-Price' and the address 'Norton Manor, Radnor', was investigated by Hall. He says that the titled family residing at Norton Hall, the Green-Prices, had never heard of a Robert Ditcher-Price

well on the site of the rectory. The canon suggested that the ghost of the former nun stole a French dictionary from the residents of Borley Rectory in the 19th century so that she could brush up on her English in order to communicate with them.

Despite some other preposterous twists in the canon's theory, Price seized on it eagerly. Hall accuses him of manufacturing and planting evidence to back it up. Part of this evidence was two French medals that Price claimed had appeared as 'apports' during his first visit to the rectory in 1929. One was a Roman Catholic confirmation medal and the other a badge or pass issued to members of the National Assembly after the revolution. Yet previously, Price had said that there was one apported medal and that it was a 'Loyola' medal. Price's faithful secretary stated that the Loyola medal was the only one she had ever seen.

Puzzling finds

Further to this case, Hall recounts how Price had excavated what he called a well in the ruined cellars of Borley Rectory in 1943, discovering a human jawbone in the soft earth. The excavation was made by lamp-light. The well turned out to be a modern concrete basin. And during the demolition of the ruins, a switch and lengths of wire were found in the cellar, though the house had never been supplied with electricity. Had Price used this equipment with a portable battery to light the cellars as he secretly buried the jawbone for later discovery?

And so Trevor Hall's book goes on, each damning fact backed by documentary evidence, much of which is from Price's own unpublished notes and correspondence. Price's accounts of psychical research projects are shown time and again to be inaccurate, or almost entirely invented, or presented over the years in different versions with contradictory details. *Search for Harry Price* certainly fulfills Colin Wilson's criterion: it shows Price as a confirmed liar and publicity seeker. The absurd experiment in which Price and Professor C. E. M. Joad conducted a magical ceremony in the Harz mountains in Germany for a regiment of press photographers more than proves the latter. But even more, the revelations indicate that he was a fraud.

But does the tarnishing of Price's character necessarily mean that the haunting of Borley Rectory was fraudulent? From the year the rectory was built in 1863 until 1929, when Price first became interested in it, stories circulating in the area had seemed to suggest paranormal happenings. Furthermore, from 1930 to 1937 Price visited Borley only once, and yet at least 2000 allegedly paranormal incidents were recorded during that time. In a year straddling 1937 and 1938, when Price rented the empty rectory and recruited a team of independent witnesses through an advertisement in *The Times* to live there with him, several incidents were reported in Price's absence. Finally, between Price's residency and 27 February 1939, when the rectory was 'mysteriously' destroyed by fire at midnight, odd events occurred.

So, regardless of Price's role, was Borley Rectory in fact the 'most haunted house in England?'

Large, dark and ugly, Borley Rectory seemed to invite haunting. And with the arrival of ghost hunter Harry Price, it became a hive of paranormal activity. New discoveries began to emerge or was someone helping things along?

ALTHOUGH IT SERVED as rectory to the 12th-century Borley church, which stood amid ancient gravestones on the opposite side of the Sudbury road, the ' most haunted house in England' was only 76 years old when it burned to the ground in the winter of 1939. Borley Rectory was an ugly two-storey building of red brick, its grounds dotted with tall trees that cast gloom on many of its 23 rooms. It was built in 1863 by the Reverend Henry D. E. Bull, who was both a local landowner and rector of Borley church, to house his wife and 14 children.

Immediately behind and to one side of the house lay a farmyard bounded by a cottage, stabling and farm buildings. When an extra wing was added to the house in 1875, a small central courtyard resulted. The dining-room fireplace was carved with figures of monks, a decoration suggesting that the Rev. Bull may have believed a local legend that a 13th-century monastery had once occupied the spot. One of the monks from this monastery gave rise to the first ghost story about the site. He was said to have eloped with a nun from a convent at Bures, some 8 miles (13 kilometres) away. But the couple were caught and executed, he being beheaded and she walled up in the convent. And their ghosts haunted the area. The roots of this picturesque tale were cut away in 1938 by a letter from the Essex Archaeological Society to Sidney Glanville, one of the most diligent and

Above: the Reverend Henry (Harry) Bull and the choir of Borley church. Like his father before him, Harry Bull perpetuated the story of the haunting of the rectory by a nun

Below: the gloomy 23-room rectory as seen from the tower of the church

Borley: the tension mounts

Above: the summerhouse in which Harry Bull dozed away his last years. He claimed that he saw the ghostly nun and other apparitions while he rested here

honest volunteer investigators for the ghost hunter and author Harry Price. It stated that neither the monastery nor the nunnery had ever existed.

However, there is evidence that both the Rev. Henry Bull and his son and successor as rector, the Rev. Harry Bull, enjoyed telling the story. It gained currency particularly among Sunday school children, many of whom presumably grew up believing it – in view of its source – to be 'gospel'.

Before this first 'nun's tale' was replaced by a later version, reports grew that various members of the Bull family – notably two of the sisters, Millie and Ethel – had seen a shadowy figure in the long rectory garden moving across what then became known as the 'nun's walk'. This route followed the path of an underground stream, along which clouds of gnats were inclined to drift on warm summer evenings. The two sisters told Price that they had seen the nun in July 1900, adding only that it was 'evening' and 'sunlit' – so no one can be sure it was not a formation of gnats. A later rector, the Rev. G. Eric Smith, told of being startled by a 'white figure' that turned out to be the smoke from a bonfire, while V. C. Wall, a *Daily Mirror* reporter, saw a similar apparition that proved to be the maid.

The Bull family lived at Borley Rectory in basic discomfort – without gas, electricity or mains water – for almost 65 years. When his father died in 1892, Harry took over as rector and continued to live in the house with his numerous siblings. At least three of the family remained in occupation until Harry's death in June 1927. He himself moved across the road to Borley Place when he married in 1911, but returned to the rectory in 1920, presumably after his wife's death.

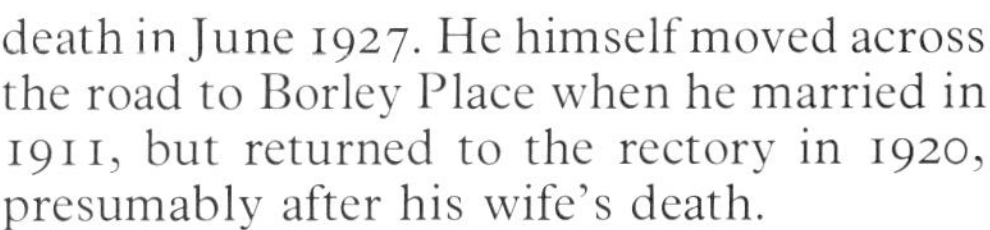

Despite the architectural gloom of their surroundings, the younger Bulls seem to have been a lively crowd, according to the testimony of friends and acquaintances who contacted researchers in the late 1940s and early 1950s. The house had curious acoustics that lent themselves to practical jokes. According to Major the Hon. Henry Douglas-Home of the Society for Psychical Research, footsteps in the courtyard at the rear of the house and voices in the adjoining cottage could clearly be heard in the rectory, along with the noise made by the hand pump in the stable yard. These provided plenty of thumps and groans, he said. Another source told researchers that the young Bull sisters took a delight in telling maids that the house was 'haunted', and one old servant mentioned that after being primed in this way by Edith Bull, she had heard 'shuffling' noises outside her room.

As he grew older, Harry Bull added his own contributions to the village gossip. He appears to have had narcolepsy, a condition in which the sufferer is always drowsy, and took to sleeping for most of the day in a summerhouse. After his snoozes, he claimed he had seen the nun, heard the phantom coach in which she had eloped with the monk, and spoken to an old family retainer named Amos, who had been dead for years. By 1927, when Bull died and the family finally left the rectory, it had become a 'haunted house' in local imagination. This reputation was probably enhanced as the house lay empty and dilapidated for over a year.

On 2 October 1928, the new rector of Borley arrived with his wife. The Rev. G. Eric Smith had spent his early married life in India, but following his wife's serious illness there, he decided to return home, take holy orders, and seek a living. Desperation may

Below: the place where the ghost of the nun disappears after her walk in the rectory garden. Up to this point – and where she walks – the stream is underground

have been setting in when he accepted Borley, for he took it on trust and both he and his wife were dismayed when they discovered the condition of the rectory.

To add to their troubles during the first winter, the Smiths soon heard that the house was 'haunted'. The 'ghosts' themselves did not trouble them, however. As Mrs Smith was to write in a letter to the *Church Times* in 1945, neither of them thought the house haunted by anything but 'rats and local superstition'.

Smith's main worry was that the more nervous of his parishioners were unwilling to come to the rectory for evening meetings. When he failed to talk them out of their fears, he took what was perhaps the fatal step of writing to the editor of the *Daily Mirror* to ask for the address of a psychical research society. He hoped that trained investigators could solve the mystery in a rational way and allay the fears of the locals.

Instead, the editor sent a reporter, V. C. Wall, and on Monday, 10 June 1929, he filed the first sensational newspaper account about Borley Rectory. His story talked of 'Ghostly figures of headless coachmen and a nun, an old-time coach, drawn by two bay horses, which appears and vanishes mysteriously, and dragging footsteps in empty rooms....'

The *Mirror* editor also telephoned Price, who made his first visit two days later. With Price's arrival, 'objective phenomena' began for the first time. Almost as soon as he set foot on the premises, a flying stone smashed a window, an ornament shattered in the hallway, showers of apports – pebbles, coins, a medal and a slate – rattled down the main stairs. The servants' bells jangled of their own accord and keys flew out of their locks. During a seance held in the Blue Room – a bedroom overlooking the garden with its 'nun's walk' – rappings on a wall mirror supposedly made by the late Harry Bull were heard by Price and his secretary, Wall, the Smiths, and two of the Bull sisters who were visiting the house.

Price made several trips to the house during the weeks that followed, each visit being accompanied by strange phenomena that were duly reported in the *Daily Mirror* by Wall.

The results were predictable: far from quelling his parishioners' fears, the Rev. Smith had not only unwittingly increased them but added another dimension to his catalogue of woes. The district was invaded by sightseers night and day. Coach parties were organised by commercial companies and the Smiths found themselves virtually under siege. On 14 July, distressed by the ramshackle house and its unwelcome visitors, they moved to Long Melford. Smith ran the parish from there before taking another living in Norfolk in April 1930.

Price must have been made uneasy on at least two occasions at Borley. One of these was when some coins and a Roman Catholic medallion featuring St Ignatius Loyola 'materialised' and fell to the ground at about the same time as some sugar lumps flew through

Below: the spectral nun and the phantom coach haunting the site of Borley Rectory (seen on the left). In some versions of the story, the drivers of the coach were beheaded – which accounts for the headless figures in this picture. The nun was eloping with a monk, who was hanged when the two were caught. She was bricked up into a wall, we are told

Bottom: pointing out the place where the apparitional coach vanishes

the air. When they were picked up, they were, recalled Mrs Smith, strangely warm to the touch, as if from a human hand. Her maid Mary Pearson, a known prankster, gave her the solution: 'That man threw that coin,' she explained, 'so I threw some sugar.' An even more farcical incident marked the second near-miss for Price during a further seance in the Blue Room. Heavy footsteps were heard outside, accompanied by the slow rumble of shutters being drawn back. In the doubtless stunned hush that followed, Price asked aloud if it were the spirit of the Rev. Harry Bull. A guttural voice, clearly recognisable as that of a local handyman, replied: 'He's dead, and you're daft.'

Rats, Mrs Smith later averred, lay behind the bell ringing – the bell wires ran along rafters under the roof. As for a mysterious light that 'appeared' in an upstairs window, it was well-known locally as a trick reflection of light from the railway carriages that passed along the valley.

For six months after the Smiths left Borley parish, the rectory was unoccupied once more. Then on 16 October 1930 the Rev. Harry Bull's cousin, Lionel A. Foyster, moved in as the new rector. The Rev. Foyster, a man in his early fifties, had moved back home from his previous post as rector of Sackville, Nova Scotia, which he had held between 1928 and 1930. He suffered from rheumatism but, despite his painful illness, he was a kindly and well-liked man. He was deeply devoted to his attractive wife Marianne, who was 31, and their adopted daughter Adelaide, a child of about two and a half.

During the five years that the Foysters lived at Borley, an estimated 2000 separate 'incidents' occurred, most of them within a period of about 14 months. These included voices, footsteps, objects being thrown, apparitions and messages scribbled in pencil on walls. It is probably true to say that with one possible exception, none of these could be attributable to Harry Price, who visited the rectory only once while the Foysters were there. The day after his visit, on 15 October 1931, he wrote one of the few straightforward statements he was ever to make on the Borley mystery in a letter to a colleague: '... although psychologically, the case is of great value, psychically speaking there is nothing in it.'

Six months had elapsed since the Smiths' departure and the Foysters' arrival, and in that time Borley Rectory had become more dilapidated than ever. According to her husband's cousins, the Bulls, Mrs Foyster hated the place from the moment she saw it. She made no friends locally, and her only companion, apart from Lionel, was a family friend, François D'Arles, a French-Canadian much nearer her own age. He rented the cottage at the rear of the house, and SPR investigators got the impression that he dominated the household. By 1932 Marianne Foyster and D'Arles had opened a flower shop together in London and returned to Borley only at weekends, the implication being that they had become lovers. Mrs Foyster often behaved oddly, if not hysterically, fainting when frustrated. Once she flung herself on her knees before assembled investigators to pray to St Anthony for 'vindication' when no manifestations were forthcoming – as though she expected to be able to produce them.

When the 'hauntings' of Borley Rectory began again shortly after the Foysters' arrival, the villagers accused Marianne Foyster – to her face – of being behind them.

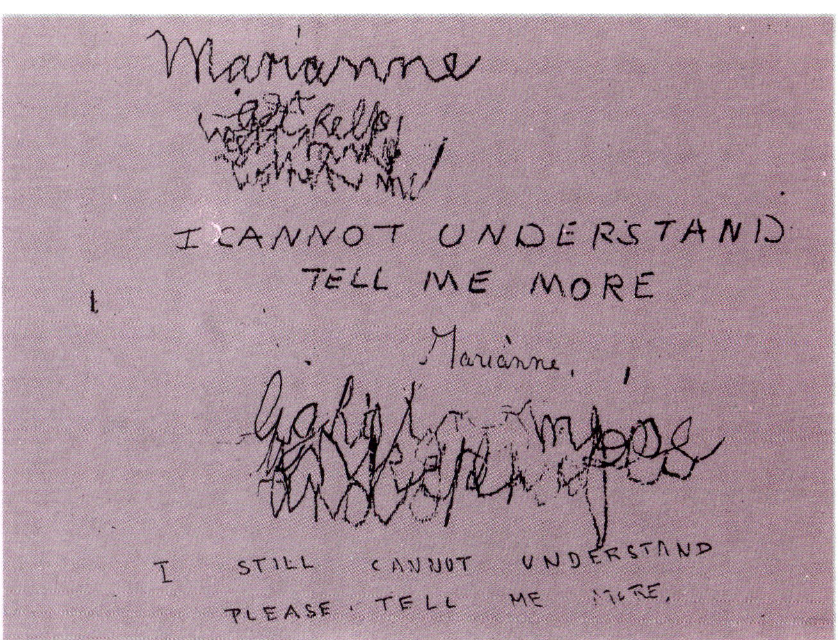

Top: an example of the 'spirit' writing on the wall of the rectory, addressed to Marianne Foyster. Paranormal phenomena increased when the Foysters came to live at Borley

Above: Harry Price at work in his own laboratory. His investigation of the Borley haunting is one of the most controversial of his career

Left: the foot of the main stairs of the rectory, scene of a rain of apports – coins, pebbles and other materialised objects. This happened almost immediately after Price arrived

Borley in ruins?

Writing on the walls, bells that ring themselves, apparitions and mysterious fires – such were the non-stop paranormal phenomena that occurred after the Foyster family moved into Borley Rectory. The question was, were they real?

Above: Borley Rectory, which seemed to reach the peak of its haunting when Marianne Foyster lived there. It is still an open question as to whether she created the events herself. If so, was it because she suffered from an hysteric disorder she could not control – like Esther Cox in the similar Amherst case? Or did she produce the phenomena through PK?

IN 1878 A YOUNG WOMAN named Esther Cox became the centre of 'mysterious manifestations' at her sister's home in Amherst, Nova Scotia. Esther saw apparitions visible to no one else. Objects were thrown, furniture was upset, small fires broke out in the house and messages addressed to the girl were found scribbled on the walls. The 'hauntings' became the subject of a book, *The haunted house: a true ghost story . . . the great Amherst mystery* (1879) by Walter Hubbell. The book was a huge success, running through 10 editions and selling over 55,000 copies. But in 1919 the American Society for Psychical Research printed a 'critical study' by Dr Walter F. Prince, suggesting that the Amherst case was not in fact a poltergeist manifestation. Prince said it was all trickery by Esther Cox while in a state of dissociation, or conversion hysteria.

The township of Amherst is about 5 miles (8 kilometres) from the equally small community of Sackville, where another of Esther Cox's married sisters lived and where, 50 years afterwards, the Reverend Lionel Foyster and his wife Marianne lived. The Foysters would have heard of the Amherst case as surely as anyone living in, say, Sudbury today would have heard of the Borley mystery. The fact that Foyster used the pseudonym 'Teed' when writing of the happenings at Borley Rectory during his stay there offers what is tantamount to proof that he not only knew of the Amherst case but was familiar with its details: the unusual name 'Teed' was the married name of Esther Cox's sister. It seems likely, therefore, that his wife also knew of the case, though whether she made deliberate – if unconscious – use of it for her own behaviour is a matter for conjecture. The resemblance between both cases is, in fact, striking; Dingwall, Goldney and Hall in *The haunting of Borley Rectory* offer no less than 19 points of general concurrence, including the ringing of bells, throwing of objects, setting of small fires, and mysterious messages written on walls.

For example, a short time after Marianne Foyster arrived at Borley and took such a dislike to the place, she began to 'see apparitions'. No one else did. Shortly afterwards

Below: the cottage that was once part of the Borley Rectory property and in which François D'Arles lived

the manifestations, so similar to the Amherst case, began. Her husband, loyal and devoted, answered villagers who accused her of faking that he could not see the visions because 'he wasn't psychic', but in her 'defence' he began to keep a rough record of events. This was not perhaps as helpful as he hoped it might be because, as he admitted, much of it was written later and many things were confused.

In October 1931, in answer to a plea from the Bull sisters, Harry Price returned to Borley once more. It is interesting to speculate on the motives behind the Bulls' concern: perhaps because they knew the source of the pranks and hoaxes during their own tenancy, they suspected the genuineness of the new 'haunting'. The same could be said of Harry Price, for he returned from his visit convinced that Mrs Foyster was directly responsible for fraud.

In their examination of the alleged phenomena, Dingwall, Goldney and Hall analysed the incidents described in Foyster's first record, which he later elaborated upon. Treating the constant bell ringing as a single phenomenon, they isolated 103 different instances. Of these, 99 depended totally on Mrs Foyster's sincerity, three were readily attributable to natural causes, and only one was in any way 'inexplicable'.

Among the most suspicious incidents was the appearance of pencilled writings on the walls. About seven messages appeared during the Foysters' tenancy, most of them addressed to Marianne and appealing for 'light, mass, prayers'. Another, not noted by Price in his Borley books, spelled 'Adelaide', the name of the Foysters' adopted daughter. All the messages were in a childish scribble. Little Adelaide may have been responsible for one or both of the 'mysterious' small fires that broke out in the rectory, for she was caught on at least one occasion trying to set fire to bedclothes.

In 1933 when the Foysters went on leave for six months, they left Canon H. Lawton as locum. Nothing untoward happened though the canon, like Major Douglas-Home of the Society for Psychical Research, noted the curious acoustics of the house and surroundings. In any case, by that time Mrs Foyster was spending most of her time in London with François D'Arles at their flower shop. An exorcism by a group of Spiritualists the previous year, when Marianne and François first left to open their shop, seemed to have put paid to what the Foysters cosily called 'the goblins'. Or was it that Marianne Foyster was no longer on the premises?

In October 1935 the Foysters left Borley. When the Reverend A.C. Henning was appointed five months later, he chose to live elsewhere, and since his time the rectors of Borley have lived at Liston or Foxearth

Below: the ghost hunter Harry Price (left) and Mrs K. M. Goldney of the Society for Psychical Research (right) pose with the Foyster family at Borley Rectory. The Foysters' adopted child Adelaide and an unidentified playmate complete the picture

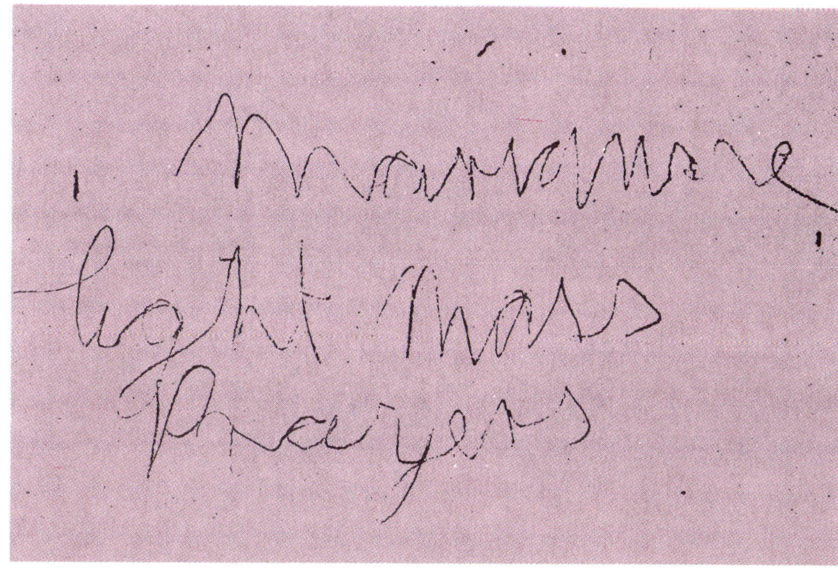

Bottom: one of several messages that appeared on the walls of the rectory. All of them were scribbled in pencil in a childish hand and were mostly addressed to Marianne Foyster

One of Price's 48 volunteer investigators takes a break from his duties at the rectory. Price rented Borley for a year and gathered a team of 'observers' through an advertisement in *The Times* to work with him there. He did not ask for experience in psychical research, but required his volunteers to have 'leisure and intelligence' and to be 'critical and unbiased'

rectories, parishes amalgamated with Borley since the 1930s.

But the battered, drama-ridden old house had still another four years of life to run. On 19 May 1937 Harry Price rented the rectory, and a week later inserted an advertisement in *The Times* asking for 'responsible persons of leisure and intelligence, intrepid, critical and unbiased' to form a rota of observers at the house. If, he later stated, they 'knew nothing about psychical research, so much the better'.

As has been pointed out by Price's critics, ignorance of psychical research is a curious requirement for a team of ghost hunters, but could make it easier to use their 'experiences' to build a good story.

If Harry Price and Marianne Foyster had used fraud for their own personal ends, another trickster who came on the scene in November 1938 was working for purely financial gain. He was Captain William Hart Gregson, who bought Borley Rectory six months after Price's tenancy expired. He immediately asked Price's advice about organising coach trips to see his new property and broadcast on the radio, recounting several minor 'phenomena'. But his coach tour plans were brought to an abrupt end at midnight on 27 February 1939 when fire gutted the building, leaving only a few walls, charred beams, and chimney stacks standing.

Sidney Glanville, one of Price's volunteer researchers of impeccable reputation, said that at a seance at the Glanville home, an entity named 'Sunex Amures' had threatened to burn down Borley Rectory. But the real cause was flatly stated by Sir William Crocker in his autobiography *Far from humdrum: a lawyer's life* (1967). Crocker, a distinguished barrister, and Colonel Cuthbert Buckle, an insurance adjuster, investigated the claim made by Gregson on behalf of the insurers. Crocker states: 'We repudiated his impudent claim for "accidental loss by fire" . . . pleading that he had fired the place himself.'

'Bare-faced hocus pocus'

The ruins of Borley Rectory were finally demolished in the spring of 1944 and the site levelled. An orchard and three modern bungalows now occupy the spot. During the demolition, Price took a *Life* magazine photographer and researcher Cynthia Ledsham to Borley, and by sheer fluke, the photographer captured on film a brick that was apparently 'levitated' by unseen forces – but was in fact thrown by a worker. *Life* published the photograph over a jokey caption, but Price, in his book *The end of Borley Rectory* (1946), claimed it as a final 'phenomenon'. Cynthia Ledsham was astounded, calling it 'the most bare-faced hocus pocus on the part of . . . Harry Price.'

The truth is that the haunting of Borley Rectory was the most bare-faced hocus pocus from start to finish, with Price feeding his craving for personal publicity from it in the most short sighted way. For, as was shown after his death, his shallow frauds could not hope to withstand investigation.

In a letter to Mr C.G. Glover in 1938, Price wrote: 'As regards your various criticisms, the alleged haunting of the rectory stands or falls not by the reports of our recent observers, but by the extraordinary happenings there of the last 50 years.'

But he wrote to Dr Dingwall in 1946 in reference to the occasion when a glass of water was 'changed' into ink: 'I agree that Mrs Foyster's wine [*sic*] trick was rather crude, but if you cut out the Foysters, the Bulls, the Smiths, etc., something still remains.' It is then logically left that the 'something' is the 'reports of our recent observers'.

As Dingwall, Goldney and Hall said: 'If one wished to dispose of the Borley hauntings on one small piece of paper merely by reference to Price's privately expressed opinions of the evidence', it would be necessary only to quote the two letter extracts in juxtaposition. However, one great irony remains. Despite the demolition of Price's pack of lies, ghost hunters of the 1960s and 1970s doggedly persisted in investigating the area. And they may just have stumbled on something truly paranormal – not at the rectory site, but in Borley church itself.

No end to Borley

Were Harry Price, his detractors and his defenders, chasing ghosts in the wrong place by concentrating on Borley Rectory? This chapter examines a case for a genuine haunting across the road at Borley church, under investigation since the 1970s

IN ALL HIS BORLEY investigations and writings, Harry Price paid scant attention to the 12th-century church itself. He was aware of a story, told to him by Ethel Bull in 1929, that coffins in the Waldegrave family vault under the church had been mysteriously moved at some time during the 19th century, but he made little attempt to follow up the matter. Price may have missed his real chance to confront the paranormal. For, since the early 1970s, unexplained events in and around the church – many of them recorded on tape – have proved to be far more baffling than anything that happened in the old rectory.

The manor of 'Barlea' – the Anglo-Saxon for 'boar's pasture' – was mentioned in Domesday Book, when a wooden church served the locality. The south wall of the present church contains remnants of the flint and rubble building erected in the 12th century. The chancel, the north wall of the nave, and the west tower were added in the 15th century, followed a hundred years later by the red brick south porch.

Below: Borley church, the major part of which was constructed in the 15th century. Should the many who investigated the Borley Rectory hauntings have looked here instead?

In the little churchyard itself, planted around with clipped yews and horse chestnut trees, lie the graves of the Bull family. Vandals have broken the stone cross on that of the Rev. Harry Bull, the Victorian rector who drowsed away his last days in the summerhouse and reported seeing a ghostly nun and phantom coach. Geoffrey Croom-Hollingsworth, who runs a small psychical research group at Harlow, Essex, believes from his investigations that the cause of the rector's death in 1927 was syphilis. Advanced syphilis is accompanied by narcolepsy, a constant drowsiness, during which the sufferer hallucinates – a fact that would seem to explain the rector's 'visions' neatly. But Croom-Hollingsworth does not think this is the whole answer, for he and an assistant, Roy Potter, claim to have observed the phantom nun themselves for a period of about 12 minutes.

Croom-Hollingsworth came upon the Borley controversy in the 1960s and decided to examine the facts himself. He and his group began a series of vigils at Borley. Like subsequent investigators, they chose to keep watch at night to avoid interruption. Over a period of years, in differing weather conditions and at different times of year, they heard an assortment of noises: raps, heavy panting and the sound of furniture being moved. On one occasion while in the orchard, something huge and dark, 'like an animal', approached them between the fruit trees and banged loudly on the fence.

On another night, at about 3 a.m., the group heard 'laughter and merriment . . . which seemed to be coming up the road towards Borley church'. The night was misty, but there was sufficient light to see that nobody was in the roadway. Assuming that the voices were those of late-night revellers, but puzzled by the direction of the sound, Roy Potter got into his car and coasted down the road towards Long Melford with his engine off. He met nobody. Using his walkie-talkie link with Croom-Hollingsworth, he arranged the experiment of shouting at various points along the Long Melford road to see if the sound carried. The listeners in the churchyard heard nothing. In an attempt to record similar noises, a tape recorder was set up in the porch of the church, while the group kept watch from a distance. Nobody was seen to enter the porch, but the group heard a loud crash and found the tape recorder 'pretty well battered'. The tape had been torn from its reels and lay in a tangle.

Previous page: the Enfield Parapsychical Research Group at Borley church. Ronald R. Russell (far right), a founding member, leans towards Price's side in the controversy over Borley's hauntings. But the group have found the church itself of most interest and have done many tests with cameras and sound equipment (right)

Above right: the vandalised grave of the Reverend Harry Bull in Borley churchyard. Harry's father built the nearby rectory that became famous as 'the most haunted house in England', so drawing attention away from the church

But it was the sighting of the nun that convinced the Harlow group that something was indeed strange about Borley. One clear night, Croom-Hollingsworth was standing in the orchard, looking towards the 'nun's walk':

> Suddenly I saw her quite clearly, in a grey habit and cowl as she moved across the garden and through a hedge. I thought 'is somebody pulling my leg?' Roy was out in the roadway, the nearest of the group, and I shouted to him. The figure had disappeared into a modern garage, and I thought that was that, but

BBC as a basis for a television programme, are, Densham says, 'quite baffling'.

The first taping began at midnight during the winter months. After the church was carefully examined and searched, a cassette player was placed by the altar and the investigators sat at the other end of the church. The tape picked up a series of bumps and raps. Next, two tape recorders were locked up in the church, one by the altar and the other halfway down the aisle. Both picked up the unmistakable sound of a heavy door being opened and slammed shut, complete with the squeaking of a bolt. Neither the porch door nor the smaller chancel door had been opened – the researchers had kept watch on the church from outside – and examination showed that the chancel door bolt did not squeak.

The following week Densham and his team started their vigil at 12.30 a.m. They set up a sophisticated stereo tape with two high quality microphones, again placing one near the altar and the other halfway down the aisle; an additional cassette machine was positioned in front of the altar. Then half the team were locked into the church and the other half kept watch in the churchyard.

'Suddenly there was a curious change in the atmosphere,' said Densham. 'One of the team felt as if he was being watched, and we all felt very cold.' During the next few minutes the tapes picked up a clatter, as if something had been thrown down the aisle. There were also knockings, rappings, the sound of the door opening again – although both doors remained locked and bolted – and, chillingly, the sound of a human sigh. Afterwards, the team found that the small cassette recorder had jammed, and the tape

> as Roy joined me we both saw her come out of the other side. She approached to about 12 feet [3 metres] from us, and we both saw her face, that of an elderly woman in her sixties, perhaps. We followed her as she seemed to glide over a dry ditch as if it wasn't there, before she disappeared into a pile of building bricks. Neither of us was frightened. It was an odd sensation, but peaceful and tranquil.

Not surprisingly in view of his experiences, Croom-Hollingsworth has little time for the critics who point to the discrepancies in Price's account of the haunting. On the other hand, he says,

> I don't give a damn if Price invented things or not. The basic question is – is the place haunted? And you can take it from me it is. I have invented nothing. Roy and I saw the nun quite clearly for a period of about 12 minutes. . . .

Croom-Hollingsworth's determination impressed Denny Densham, a film director and cameraman. In 1974 he got permission to experiment with tape recorders in the church. The results, which were used by the

Above: the Waldegrave tomb, memorial to an old and influential Borley family. Local gossip had it that the Waldegrave coffins in the vault under the church were 'mysteriously moved' in the 19th century

Right: one of the stained glass windows of the church, dedicated to the Reverend Henry Bull. His retelling of the story of the ghostly nun of Borley Rectory gave a boost to the reputation of his family home as a haunted house

had been extracted and tangled up, as the Croom-Hollingsworth tape had been.

In July, the party visited Borley again. At 1.45 a.m., they felt a change in the atmosphere.

> We all felt watched, and a curious tingling sensation was felt; oddly enough the machines seemed to pick up a lot of static at this point. We recorded stealthy sounds near the altar, the sound of the door shutting again, a crash as of something being knocked over, and then the sound of hollow, heavy footsteps, like those of a very large man walking by the altar rail. We could not reproduce them normally: the floor there is of stone, heavily carpeted.

The observers then saw a glow of light near the chancel door, followed by a terrifying grunt. On this, their final visit, the team saw pinpoints of light in the curtains by one door, and heard the sound of a heavy crash. Densham said:

> Frankly, I am at a loss to explain what goes on at Borley. We made every effort to ensure that our legs weren't being pulled, and the tapes were new and untampered with. No theory I have tried to put forward seems to pan out. We tried leaving pencil and paper in the church, asked the thing to rap and so on, but it doesn't seem to be trying to communicate, unless the damage to the tapes and the throwing of invisible objects in our direction meant that it resented our presence. One's left with the feeling that whatever causes the phenomena is indifferent to or perhaps unaware of observers.

'Ectoplasm' in the churchyard

Since that summer of 1974, one of the most regular researchers at Borley has been Ronald R. Russell, a member of the Enfield Parapsychical Research Group and professional photographer. Frank Parry, an electrical engineer, and John Fay, a mechanical engineer, usually work with him. Russell has achieved odd results while taking photographs of the area with an Agfa CC21 camera, in which the film is contained in a cassette and processed in the Agfa laboratory.

> Sandwiched between perfectly normal frames we got 'ectoplasmic' stuff in the churchyard, shadows where no shadows should be, and a thin light near the north door. As a photographer I'm at a loss to explain this as camera or film malfunction.

Parry has used a graphic analyser, an eight-channel recording machine with slider controls that adjust pitch and level, cut out interference, and enable its operator to 'pinpoint' sounds. As Russell said:

> We have recorded hundreds of extraordinary noises, footsteps, crashes and so on. On one occasion we located a centre of disturbance near the Waldegrave tomb; it was tangible, like a swirling column of energy. When you passed your hand through it you felt a sort of crackle, like static electricity. On another occasion we heard a deep, grunting voice, which reminded me irresistibly of Lee Marvin singing *Wandering Star*.

The altar in Borley church. In 1974 some strange sounds – including raps, crashes and mysterious footsteps – were picked up here on a cassette recorder

Russell is inclined to side with the Price faction on Borley, though he concedes that Price may have embellished facts.

> I think there may be three basic factors at work here. First, the nun. There would be nothing odd about a nun in the household of a Catholic family like the Waldegraves. Perhaps the apparition which Mr Croom-Hollingsworth saw is simply a psychic record of some such person. Secondly, there seems to be some sort of power concentrated in the church itself. It is on the intersection of two ley lines, and when you try dowsing in the church the rod practically twists from your hands. Thirdly, I would suggest that the power is boosted by the presence of observers, and also that it waxes and wanes with the seasons; in January phenomena are sporadic, while in August they seem to be at full flood.

The church authorities are non-committal, preferring to avoid discussion of the topic. But in the parish guidebook, under the heading 'ghosts', is a footnote:

> There are, of course, those who suggest the church itself is haunted. Many old churches and buildings have noises and chill areas which some would classify as ghostly, but those who have lived long in the village and we who worship in the church have not experienced anything which would support such thoughts. . . . Visitors should please remember that this is God's house and treat it with reverence.

Beware – PK at work

Top: the entrance to lawyer Adam's office at Königstrasse 13 in the quiet Bavarian town of Rosenheim (above). 'No 13' was to prove an unlucky address for Herr Adam as the increasing ferocity of the poltergeist there made work almost impossible

When a Bavarian lawyer started to have trouble with his telephone, he little suspected that his quiet office was about to be plagued by a massive poltergeist attack, resulting in one of the most startling cases of psychokinesis ever reported

A LAWYER'S OFFICE IN ROSENHEIM, Bavaria, was the unlikely setting for a poltergeist case that completely altered public opinion on the subject of poltergeists in Germany.

Armed with introductions from Hans Bender, director of the Freiburg Institute of Parapsychology, the authors travelled with a camera team to Rosenheim in the spring of 1975 to make a television documentary on the case for BBC television. Arriving at the centre of town, we sought out Königstrasse 13, a tall building in which various professional men had their consulting rooms, and which had been the scene of the notorious poltergeist activities we had come to investigate. They had centred on the office of a lawyer named Adam.

Herr Adam told us that the events that were to become so famous began quietly enough in the summer of 1967, when telephone malfunctions were reported by office staff. Calls to the office on Rosenheim 1233 had been interrupted by clicks or cut off, and sometimes all four receivers would ring at once although the line was dead. The malfunctions had become too frequent to overlook, and the office manager, Johannes Engelhard, called in repair men from Siemens, the company that had installed the equipment – a junction box and four telephones.

The Siemens engineers worked in the

office for several weeks, testing wiring and equipment. Although they found no faults, they replaced the receivers and junction box – but, as this did not improve matters, they called in the post office.

Early in October, the post office replaced the Siemens equipment with official post office telephones. They installed a meter so that, as they were made, calls could be recorded visibly in the office on a counter, with a similar meter at the telephone exchange to provide an official record. At the same time, Herr Adam asked his staff, the office manager Johannes Engelhard, two office clerks and a part-time worker, to make a note of their calls.

On 5 October 1967, Adam and Engelhard were amazed to see the meter register a call although no one in the office was using the telephone. On 19 October, the same thing happened while Adam was with accountant Dr Schmidt, who produced an affidavit for Adam to show the post office. Comparing the records from his own meter, the meter at the exchange and the notes of his staff, Adam realised that these two incidents were by no means isolated. Dozens of undialled calls had been registered. The post office insisted that all the calls had been made in the normal way and, even more peculiar, they had all been made to the speaking clock.

A row broke out between the post office and Herr Adam. Adam pointed out that all his staff had watches and could hear the chimes of at least two church clocks, and could therefore keep a record of the timing of their telephone calls. Furthermore, no one was ever alone in the office, and it was ridiculous to suppose that so many calls could have been made unnoticed by anyone.

Below: trouble with the telephone was the first sign of poltergeist activity in Herr Adam's office. No mechanical or electrical fault could be found with the instrument, but massive bills were run up – and not, it seemed, by any of the employees. When records of the calls made were checked (bottom) it was discovered that someone – or some*thing* – had been making persistent calls to the speaking clock. The odd thing was that more calls were made than it was physically possible to dial in the time available. What could be making them?

Between 7.42 and 7.57 a.m. on 20 October 1967, 46 telephone calls were registered to the speaking clock. Adam further pointed out that although at least 17 seconds are needed to dial and connect with the speaking clock, even if one does not wait to hear the time, the post office claimed that as many as six calls a minute had been made, and continued to send enormous bills. Nevertheless, on 31 October, they replaced the telephones again. This time, the dials were locked and only Herr Adam had a key.

This step made no difference, and on 8 November Herr Adam was extremely angry to receive another huge bill that did not correspond with the records at all. He issued an accusation – against person or persons unknown – of fraud or embezzlement; it began: 'For several months my telephone installation has been so disturbed that a regular telephone call is impossible.'

Addicted to the time

In the spring of 1975, Adam showed us a sheaf of statements from the post office in which 0119, the number of the speaking clock, appeared over and over again. 'In five weeks,' he said, 'the speaking clock has been connected between 500 and 600 times. In one day, 80 times. I was very angry with the post office; I even wanted to found an association for the protection of the subscriber.' However, Adam soon had disturbances of a different nature to deal with.

On 20 October 1967, the office lights suddenly went out with a bang. Herr Bauer, an electrician from Stern's, a local firm, was called in to repair them. He examined the lights and found that each fluorescent tube had been turned 90° in its socket and disconnected. He had finished replacing the tubes and put away his ladder when there was

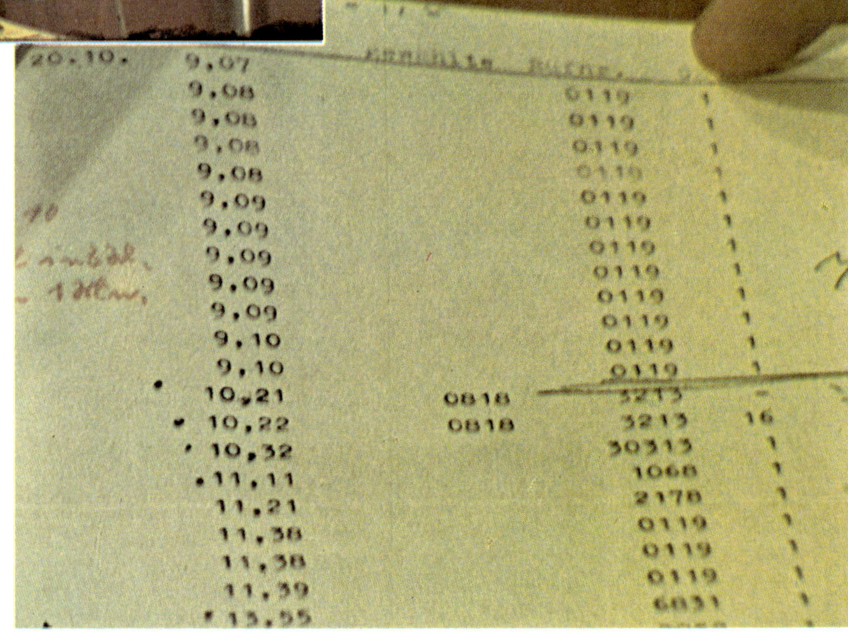

20.10.	9,07		0119	1
	9,08		0119	1
	9,08		0119	1
	9,08		0119	1
	9,08		0119	1
	9,09		0119	1
	9,09		0119	1
	9,09		0119	1
	9,09		0119	1
	9,09		0119	1
	9,10		0119	1
	9,10		0119	1
	10,21	0818	3213	–
	10,22	0818	3213	16
	10,32		30313	1
	11,11		1068	1
	11,21		2178	1
	11,38		0119	1
	11,38		0119	1
	11,39		0119	1
	13,55		6831	1

another bang. The tubes had twisted and disconnected themselves again. He was even more puzzled when the office staff told him that the automatic fuses in the office ejected themselves for no apparent reason, sometimes on all four circuits at once. Bauer began a full investigation of the office wiring and equipment, all of which he found in excellent order. He confessed to Adam: 'I was faced with a puzzle and called it "witchcraft".'

Since no fault could be found in the office, he concluded that something must be wrong with the electricity supply itself. The *Elektrizitätswerk* – German electricity board – was asked to take over the investigation. Accordingly, Paul Brunner, Auxiliary Works Manager, arrived at Adam's office on 15 November 1967.

Brunner is a small, dynamic man who impressed us with his authority and his efficiency. He was born in Rosenheim and belonged to the second generation of his family to work at the electricity board. He told us that he had had no interest in the occult, but approached Adam's office with curiosity because of its scientific challenge – yet, ironically, the official report he prepared became one of the most significant documents in paranormal research.

Right: Paul Brunner, the auxilliary works manager for the German electricity board

Below: the Unireg recorder (left) on which abnormalities in the electricity supply were detected and traced on a graph (right). At first the investigators thought that these were caused by the local electricity substation – but they found absolutely no faults there

The escalation of the Rosenheim phenomena can be seen when viewed chronologically. On Wednesday, 15 November 1967, extensive checks were run on the wiring and appliances at 13 Königstrasse, especially in Adam's flat. Everything was found to be satisfactory and short circuits were ruled out as a possible cause of the phenomena.

On Thursday, 16 November, a Siemans Unireg – an electrical instrument that shows voltage fluctuations on a single-track pen recorder – was installed at the office. Later a Tektronix plug-in unit with a storage oscilloscope was added, giving two more pen traces that showed fluctuations in the magnetic field and the noise level. A pen recorder gave a continuous read-out of current and voltage variations at selected points in the office circuitry, and the times at which they happened. The machine was sealed to prevent tampering. Over the next few weeks, it was established that abnormal deflections on the paper record occurred, but only in office hours and never at weekends. The automatic fuses were replaced with screw-in types and, to rule out trickery, these were also sealed.

On Monday, 20 November, after a 'normal' morning of twisting tubes, inexplicable voltage variations and bangs, a fluorescent tube in Adam's private office fell to the floor and shattered. At the same moment, a huge surge in the electric current – 50 amps – was registered, yet the safety fuses did not blow. On examining the read-out, Brunner was puzzled to see loops instead of the expected straight lines. Other tubes fell as the day wore on.

On Tuesday, 21 November, as a safety measure, all the fluorescent tubes in the office were replaced by normal light bulbs. More loud bangs were heard, and the photocopier

Above: Herr Adam inspects one of the lamps that began to swing wildly on 27 November 1967. The lamp on the office landing moved as much as 22 inches (55 centimetres) from its normal position

Above right: one of the more violent deflections of the trace on the Unireg recorder. No physical reason could be found for the disturbances in the electricity supply – though they did occur only during office hours, suggesting that someone on the staff was somehow responsible

began leaking chemicals. It was plugged in but not switched on. Brunner wondered if electricity were being conducted into the building through gas and water mains. The team ran a number of tests – and this possibility, too, was ruled out.

On Wednesday, 22 November, the light bulbs began to explode. The neighbourhood was searched for freak power sources. None was found.

On Thursday, 23 November, the office apartment was disconnected from the electricity mains and was connected directly by cable to the transformer, High Tension Station KII in Königstrasse.

On Friday, 24 November, Brunner thought the mystery was over. He found full deflections on the paper record, some so savage that the paper had been torn by the pen. As the meter was connected directly to KII, he thought the fault had to be there in the supply itself, and that his team had been correct in pronouncing all the electrical equipment in the office satisfactory. With relief, engineers, equipment and cable were evacuated from the office and camp was set up at KII, to pinpoint the fault. But no fault was found. Camp was reinstated at the office.

The entire supply grid of Rosenheim was checked and pronounced sound.

On Monday, 27 November, a girl was cut by flying glass from an exploding light bulb. All remaining bulbs were covered by nylon bags to prevent further accidents. Four more exploded that afternoon. Between five and six o'clock, an alarming new development forced Brunner to admit that he was dealing with something outside his experience: the lights began to swing.

The next few days were spent observing swinging lamps and trying to find an explanation for their movement: 'We leapt repeatedly up and down the floor overhead to try to make the lamps swing – without success. The traffic outside was also watched carefully, and tests were made for electrostatic charges, but none was found.'

On Thursday, 30 November, the office was severed from the mains, and power supplied instead by a 7-kilowatt generator-truck parked outside. The generator's meter showed a steady 220-volt output, yet inside the office deflections and crashes continued, lamps swung, bulbs exploded and fuses were ejected erratically.

On Thursday, 7 December, over 90 deflections were registered during the morning. Lamps swung so violently that they smashed against the ceiling, denting the plaster.

Paintings begin to twirl

To vindicate his methods and results, and to safeguard his reputation, Brunner asked the advice of Dr Karger of the Max Planck Institute of Plasma Physics, and Dr Zicha of Munich University, two of Germany's most eminent physicists. Following a suggestion from Karger, Brunner disconnected the office supply from the Unireg and placed an ordinary 1.5-volt battery across the Unireg terminals. To the astonishment of everyone, instead of registering 1.5 volts until the battery exhausted its charge, the pen began its trace at 3 volts and then zig-zagged wildly across the paper. The Unireg (which was in perfect working order) could not be monitoring the battery to which it was connected.

On Monday, 11 December, at 8.45 a.m., Brunner and his assistant, Mayr, were chatting together in the typists' office, when suddenly a painting twisted on its hook. Surprised, Brunner stretched out his hand to straighten the picture. Other paintings in the room started to rotate, some falling to the floor. The typists, who later said they had felt unusually tense that morning, were rooted to their desks with fear, but Mayr and Brunner stationed themselves at vantage points to observe this new phenomenon. They saw the first painting to move turn through 320°, its string wrapping itself round its hook.

At this point, Brunner, realising that he was out of his depth, prepared to wind up the experiments and wrote his official report. In it, he was relieved to point out the excellent state of Rosenheim's electricity supply, which had been thoroughly checked – to even Herr Adam's satisfaction; yet inexplicable voltage deflections still occurred in the office:

> It became necessary to postulate the existence of a power hitherto unknown to technology, of which neither the nature nor strength nor direction could be defined. It is an energy quite beyond our comprehension.

Alarmed by the thought that there was no apparent way of controlling this mysterious and often harmful energy, Brunner handed over the investigations to the physicists who had been monitoring the experiments.

Like Brunner, Dr Karger and Dr Zicha were fascinated by the scientific challenge of explaining the electrical disturbances in Adam's office, and they carried out an independent investigation using the most sophisticated equipment. They concentrated on finding the cause of the deflections on the meter, installing probes to examine voltage levels, magnetic fields and sound levels. Their questions and answers can be summarised as follows.

1. Were the deflections accompanied by voltage surges? *No, voltage remained constant.*
2. Were the disturbances caused by high-frequency voltage transmission from outside the office? *None measured and none found.*
3. An electrostatic charge? *No.*
4. A static magnetic field? *None detected.*
5. Loose contact in the measuring equipment's amplifier? *None found. A second machine also showed the same anomalies.*
6. Ultrasonic or infrasonic vibrations? *None found.*
7. Manual interference? *Fraud and trickery impossible.*

While measuring sound levels, they noticed that, although no sound was heard, their monitor showed a huge deflection, so they concluded that there must have been direct pressure on the crystal in the microphone. They speculated that a similar invisible force could be acting on the pen of the Unireg itself, causing the unnatural loops directly, independently of the electric current. They speculated further: the same force could be acting on the tiny springs inside the telephone, bypassing the dial. It was active only for short periods, its nature was complex and it was not electrodynamic. Known physics could not explain it.

Herr Adam sits pensively in front of the painting that turned, by itself, through almost a complete circle – to the terror of the watching office staff

A fugitive intelligence

Karger and Zicha also felt that the telephone anomalies suggested that an intelligent force was at work, because it had 'chosen' to focus its attention on the speaking clock. It was clear that the force resisted investigation, and this was another reason to speculate on the existence of an intelligence avoiding scrutiny. They prepared their report and left.

As the physicists left Adam's office, teams of investigators from other scientific fields were eager to take their place, including Professor Hans Bender from the Freiburg Institute, who began his experiments in mid December. He was joined by several policemen who had come as a result of Adam's exasperated accusation 'Against person or persons unknown', and independently these new investigators began gathering evidence. The physicists had left two important clues. First, they had suspected that a rational being was behind the phenomena and second, they confirmed that the 'poltergeist' was active in office hours only. Investigations were now centred on the office staff, Johannes Engelhard, Frau Bielmeier (the part-time assistant) and the two clerks, 17-year-old Gustel Huber and 18-year-old Annemarie Schneider.

A spirit of anger

Left: Annemarie Schneider, centre of the Rosenheim poltergeist phenomenon, photographed with her young son in April 1975

Below: a portion of the Unireg pen trace showing violent deflections beginning around 7.30 a.m. – the hour when Annemarie reported for work

Teams of investigators were mystified by the weird events at the Rosenheim lawyer's office. At length they began to suspect that the happenings were centred on a member of the office staff. The search began to discover who it was and why

AS THE PARANORMAL EVENTS in Herr Adam's office continued, work became increasingly difficult. The army of investigators and reporters who were constantly present did not make things any better, and the staff, who felt they were under continuous scrutiny, became tense and nervous. It was bad enough to have to cope with the poltergeist phenomena that continually interrupted their work, but they also had to cope with mutual suspicion each time something happened. A typical event occurred on 12 December, when Johannes Engelhard, the office manager, was opening the morning post with a knife. Frau Adam called to him from the next room, and, as he walked to the door, he heard a picture fall somewhere behind him. He spun round to see the painting lying on the floor. But that was not all. Neatly stacked on it were the letters he had been opening, together with the knife. Although the two clerks were in the office, they could not have touched the letters or the picture in the moment it took for Engelhard to turn round. All the same, he could not help suspecting that they had played a trick on him.

Soon, however, suspicion began to centre on Annemarie Schneider. She appeared to be the most tense of the office staff, and she twitched strangely whenever poltergeist activity took place. The Unireg record, which

had shown deflections only in office hours, was checked closely, and it was found that events began at 7.30 a.m. – the time that Annemarie reported for work. Hans Bender's team from the Freiburg Institute had discreetly centred investigations on her for some time. One day, one of Bender's assistants noticed a lamp swinging strangely as Annemarie walked along the corridor underneath it. It had already been decided that each of the office staff would take a short holiday, since things had been so trying. This would also enable the research team to check who, if anyone, was responsible for the phenomena. Annemarie was given first leave – and, sure enough, the office was peaceful again.

Above: the desks at which the two girl clerks in Herr Adam's office, Gustel Huber and Annemarie Schneider, worked

Below: on the afternoon of 17 January 1967 this oak cabinet, which weighs over 400 pounds (180 kilograms), moved a distance of more than a foot (30 centimetres)

Screaming and sobbing

When Annemarie returned to work on 18 December, she seemed even more tense than before, and screamed out when a lamp began to swing. The phenomena had returned with her – and with renewed intensity. Pictures swung merrily, dropping to the floor with a force that dismantled their frames, but left their glass intact. Pages flew off the calendar, and light bulbs exploded. Drawers slid out of desks, and Frau Bielmeier had to wedge one shut with a stool weighted by a typewriter. Annemarie grew more tense every day, screaming and sobbing when phenomena occurred close to her. Fortunately, the Christmas holidays arrived.

Work at the office recommenced on 1 January 1968. When everything had been normal for over a week, Adam began to hope that he was no longer Rosenheim's principal consumer of light bulbs and fluorescent tubes – until 10.30 a.m. on 9 January, when Annemarie returned.

As before, the phenomena returned with Annemarie, and as before, they had grown still more violent. Annemarie received an electric shock in her leg as she picked a picture up off the floor, and Frau Bielmeier had a cracking sensation in her ear.

The climax was reached on 17 January. With only Annemarie and Frau Adam in the office, a number of light bulbs exploded. Annemarie was so frightened that she ran upstairs to the dental surgery, where Herr Geistaller, the dentist, managed to calm her down. Later, the police came to photograph the damage. Annemarie was back at her desk, typing, when the calendar fell from the wall and desk drawers slid out. Suddenly, a metal cash box jumped out of a drawer and clattered to the floor, spilling coins and stamps everywhere. The police, who also believed Annemarie was somehow at the centre of the phenomena, began to keep a closer watch on her.

Officer Wendl was in charge of the police investigation, and he was eager to solve the case. His belief that he would eventually catch Annemarie moving objects physically was shaken that afternoon when a heavy oak cabinet moved a foot (30 centimetres). The cabinet weighed over 400 pounds (180 kilograms), and Wendl realised that, even using levers or with the help of Fräulein Huber, Annemarie could not have moved it. It had been lifted clear over the edge of the linoleum, which would have puckered had the cabinet been shoved, and it took the efforts of two burly policemen to restore it to its place. Had the cabinet episode not occurred, Wendl would have felt sure that he had proved his case, but now he doubted it. He

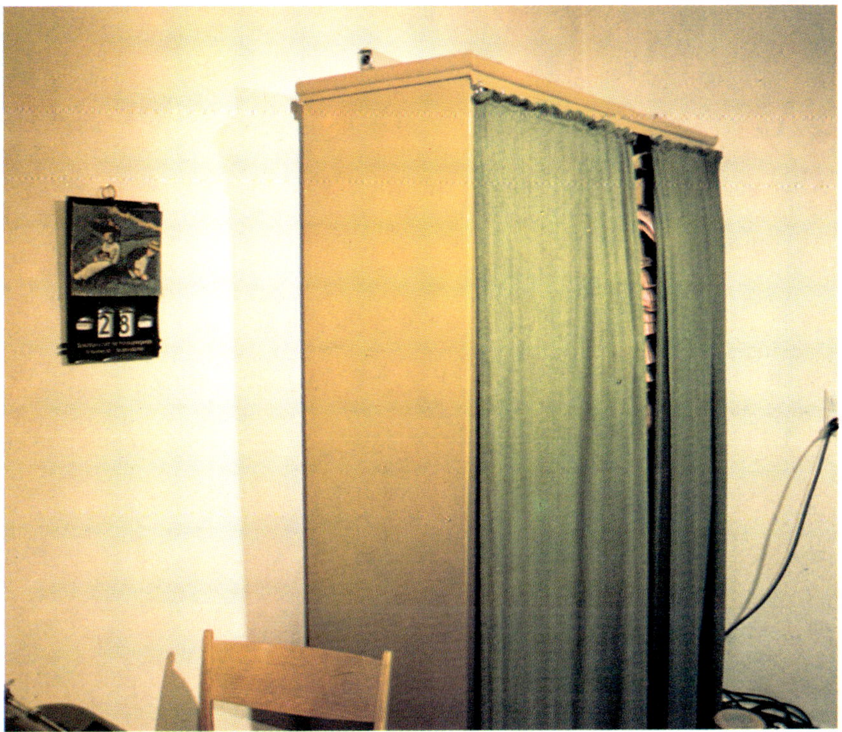

strange red patches appeared on her skin. That day, she was given further leave of absence. As she left, she noted sadly in a diary she had been asked to keep by Hans Bender: '18 January. As from today, I am on the sicklist. . . . I hope everything will proceed quickly so I can have my rest at last.'

Herr Adam lost no time. Annemarie was dismissed, and never returned to the Königstrasse office – and neither did the strange phenomena. During the poltergeist activity, the cost of the damage had amounted to 15,000 Deutschmarks, which the unfortunate Adam was obliged to pay.

Hans Bender took the opportunity of asking Annemarie to visit his Freiburg Institute so that he could do some laboratory tests and, after initial reluctance to leave home, she agreed to spend from 21 to 26 January 1968 there. A team of scientists duplicated the circuits and equipment of Adam's office, hoping to reproduce the poltergeist effects, but none of the deflections or other phenomena occurred. It seems that Annemarie could produce paranormal events only in certain specific circumstances.

Abandoning the attempt to reproduce psychokinesis, Bender tried testing Annemarie's ESP abilities. Again, nothing significant was discovered – except momentarily, when Annemarie scored highly while upset by an unpleasant memory. This seemed to confirm that stress encouraged paranormal events in her case.

Stress and frustration were seen to play a major role in Annemarie's personality. During her stay at Freiburg, she underwent extensive psychological assessment by a psychologist colleague of Bender, John Mischo. He concluded that she was unstable, irritable and suffering from frustrated rages.

was beginning to think, along with the scientists, that the ordinary laws of physics did not apply in the office, but as an extra check he organised a search for tools. None was found.

At 4.30 the same afternoon, Frau Adam arrived at the police station to inform Wendl that the cabinet had moved again. He and Officer Tischler accompanied her back to the office, which they found in chaos. The girls were almost hysterical because they had been getting electric shocks in their arms and legs all day, and before the second movement of the cabinet, tables and chairs had moved. One table had jerked along with a horrified visitor perched on it. When Frau Bielmeier left the typing room, her chair had risen, and Annemarie and Fräulein Huber's chairs both sunk. The height of the typing chairs is adjusted with a ratchet that, to prevent accidents, cannot be altered when any weight is on the seat – yet that afternoon, Professor Büchel of the Physics Institute at Pulach, near Munich, had watched Annemarie's chair descend while she was still sitting on it. She was shocked; her face blanched, then

She was unable to tolerate denial and was aggressive, although she suppressed her aggression. He believed that her constant frustrations discharged themselves through psychokinesis, via a process yet to be explained. Her own doctor had remarked on the severity of her nervous symptoms, which included hyperaemia (an excess of blood gathering in one place) and cramps. Her cramp attacks always followed the same pattern: she would cry out, and her eyes would glaze as the cramp spread. Her hands and feet would be worst affected, fingers and toes stretched painfully rigid. Muscles in her knees and hips would also flex agonisingly.

Professor Bender looked for psychological motives for the phenomena. He felt that the speaking clock was contacted as a result of Annemarie's constant desire to know when she could leave the office. Furthermore, it seems as if the damage in the office could have been prompted by aggression towards Herr Adam, as Annemarie had felt particularly tense in his office and had disliked being in his employment. Apparently, early on in the sequence of phenomena, Adam had sarcastically said: 'All we want now is for the paintings to start moving.' Annemarie was within earshot – and, moments later, the first painting started to move.

A subsequent incident confirmed, according to Bender, that Annemarie seemed to instigate psychokinesis in response to emotional problems. She seemed to Bender to be subconsciously trying to rid herself of her fiancé who, appropriately enough, was an electrical engineer. They used to go bowling together in a small alley in Raubling, a suburb on the outskirts of Rosenheim. Bowls are returned automatically, and the pins are attached to cords controlled by a system of relays that replaces them when they are knocked over. Scores are displayed on an illuminated score board.

Below: the bowling alley in Raubling, on the outskirts of Rosenheim. Annemarie used to go bowling here with her fiancé – but, after an incident in the summer of 1969 in which she apparently disrupted the electronically controlled bowling system, her fiancé broke off the engagement

Above left: Hans Bender and a colleague inspect the fluorescent light fittings that spontaneously unscrewed themselves while Annemarie Schneider was present in the office

Left: Annemarie inspects a pen trace during tests conducted by Hans Bender at the Freiburg Institute in January 1968. The results of the tests, in the sympathetic surroundings of the Institute, were disappointing: it seems that, to produce paranormal events, Annemarie had to be in a condition of stress

Annemarie continues the story:

> We had been engaged for three years and once a week we went bowling. On one occasion, the relays behaved in an eccentric way and the bowling was spoiled. I was told the relays had been put out of action, I don't know what they were talking about. My fiancé took the whole thing much too seriously and said that under the circumstances, marriage would be quite impossible.

This happened in the summer of 1969. Whatever the scientists' belief about Annemarie's subconscious wishes, she took several years to get over her broken engagement. She felt victimised, since there had been nothing to prove that the failure of the bowling mechanism was anything whatsoever to do with her.

Blamed for a death

Finally, a team of investigators went to talk directly to Annemarie. They met with her in April 1975. She turned out to be a stout, plain girl with a sad, prematurely aged face. She told them that after leaving Adam's office, she had been employed by another solicitor, Weinzier. Stories of her ability to move lamps and produce other phenomena followed her. This was the first in a long series of jobs, since the unfortunate Annemarie would always be dismissed if anything odd occurred. 'I never had influence over anything. I was very hurt indeed.' Her Bavarian colleagues still had medieval superstitions and apparently whispered that she was a witch.

She went on: 'I worked in Regenfelchen in a paper factory, and there was an accident there when a man was killed. The workers who knew who I was said, "That woman is responsible for the man's death." They didn't give me the sack from the factory immediately, they just dropped hints, so I left on my own accord. I wasn't even in the factory when it happened.'

Since that highly dubious case, there have been no new reports of paranormal happenings associated with Annemarie. She has moved to Munich where, in the anonymous surroundings of a big city, her reputation for producing psychokinetic effects has not been able to catch up with her to plague her. And perhaps this has something to do with the fact that she apparently no longer produces these effects: for, unlike most paranormal phenomena, these seemed actually to be encouraged by attention from scientists and the media. Hans Bender has pointed out that this most remarkable of cases was observed over a period of several months by more than 40 witnesses from widely ranging walks of life – office workers, electrical engineers, lawyers, scientists, psychologists and the police. For all the documentary evidence, however, *how* Annemarie produced the phenomena remains as much a mystery to scientists as ever it was.

Spook lights over America

Pale, silent, flame-like lights sometimes appear in the night in country districts and to sailors at sea. Their cause has baffled many investigators. Frank Smyth begins a series of chapters on spine-chilling hauntings with these strange tales of spook lights

THE 'WILL O' THE WISP' or 'Jack O' Lantern' was part of European ghostly lore right up until the advent of gas lighting simply because he indubitably existed. Some said he was a lost soul, treacherously leading travellers onto lonely moorland or dangerous swampland. Others said that he was an essentially benign spirit, and that if you had the courage to dig at the spot indicated by his flickering blue light on Walpurgis Night you would discover buried treasure.

But bad, good or indifferent, he was not, like some ghosts, the product of an overheated imagination: anyone who cared or dared to venture out into certain parts of the countryside after dusk could observe his eerie glow for themselves. With the coming of gas light, even country folk learned the true nature of 'Will' or 'Jack': he was simply iridescent marsh gas, similar to the stuff they now used to light their homes and streets. His mystery, if not his beauty, had vanished.

Over the years science, to the disappointment of romantics, has explained away most of the 'mystery lights' that appear in records down the centuries: airplane headlights or UFOs, shooting stars or ball lightning, reflections and refractions from the atmosphere or the surface of the sea. But not all these mysterious phenomena have succumbed to explanation so readily: some refuse to fit neatly into known patterns. Many of these seem peculiar to the United States, and American psychical researchers have jauntily dubbed them 'spook lights' – a tag that is as good as any.

One of the classic American spook light stories has its roots firmly in supernatural tradition. If any completely rational explanation exists, it has yet to be put forward, although several interesting theories have appeared over the years. The story begins in a strictly factual manner with the voyage of the *Palatine*, an elderly ship that set out from Holland in the autumn of 1752 crammed with Dutch families determined to make a

Right: some of the places in the United States where spook lights have been seen repeatedly. Many sightings are associated with rivers or bodies of water, but one is in the Arizona desert

Left: a will o' the wisp glows over the stagnant waters of a marsh, 'like a taper gleaming from some cottage window', in the words of one 19th-century account. The will o' the wisp often led the unwary onto dangerous ground

Below: terrified seamen witness the Flying Dutchman's ship, harbinger of doom. Could ghost ships and spook lights have the same natural explanation?

new life for themselves in the New World.

The vessel's scheduled destination was Philadelphia, but several factors combined to prevent it reaching its port – among them a drunken captain, a surly crew and persistent foul weather, all of which helped to keep the *Palatine* at sea for over two months. As the ship neared the New England coast, there was an argument between the officers as to the ship's exact position, and during the ensuing row the captain either fell or was thrown over the side. Heartlessly, the crew opted to save their own necks and, after robbing the passengers of what cash they could find, they put to sea in the only two lifeboats, leaving the colonists to their fate.

One morning between Christmas and New Year the *Palatine*, with its hapless passengers, grounded on the desolate coast of Block Island, about 11 miles (18 kilometres) off Long Island between Montauk and Gay Head. The local community of fishermen, accustomed to supplementing their poor livings by wrecking, evacuated the passengers but afterwards looted the ship and then set it on fire, allowing it to drift out to sea and sink. This is the story, and tradition adds that one terrified woman had hidden herself below decks. As the burning hulk was swept seaward by the tide, onlookers were horrified to see her standing at the rails screaming for help, but by that time there was nothing they could do.

Ever since then people living on the Rhode Island coast opposite Block Island have sporadically reported seeing the blazing outline of a ship during Christmas week; sometimes it appears luminous white, although in 1969 several people reported to the local newspaper, the *Westerly Sun*, that it was 'a great red fireball on the ocean.'

One of the best reports of a sighting was given by a Long Island fishing-boat owner in *Scientific American* in 1882, though he was hard-headed enough to offer an explanation that was satisfactory – and he was able to use the incident to his own profit. His boat was out after menhaden – a particularly oily fish related to the herring – with himself on board, when one of the mates said that 'he hoped we were not going off the Point, meaning Montauk. I asked him why. He seemed kind of offish, but at last let out that he had seen sailing ships sailing about in the dead of night in a dead calm.'

The mate was laughed to scorn and the fishing boat eventually made anchor in Gardiner's Bay, a few miles to the west of Block Island. That night the owner was shaken awake by the mate, who pointed anxiously out to sea.

A coaster in the spirit trade

'Sure enough, there was a big schooner about an eighth of a mile [200 metres] away, bearing down on us. There wasn't a breath of wind in the bay, but on she came at a ten-knot [18-km/h] rate, headed right for us. . . . I swung into the rigging and yelled "Schooner ahoy" and shouted to her to bear away, but in a second the white sails were right aboard of us. I shouted to the hands and made ready to jump, when, like a flash, she disappeared, and the skipper came on deck with all hands and wanted to know if we had the jimjams.'

He would have sworn, said the owner, that he had seen the Flying Dutchman's ship but a week later saw the thing again, passing round them and heading back up the bay. Apparently acting on impulse, the owner ordered the skipper to take the fishing boat after the 'phantom', at the same time setting his seine net.

'As sure as you are alive we made the biggest single haul of menhaden on record. The light to my mind was nothing more or less than the phosphorescence that hovered over the big shoal. The oil from so many millions of fish moving along was enough to produce a light; but you will find men all

The northern lights, or *aurora borealis*, glow over a lake in Manitoba, Canada. The aurora is caused by electrically charged particles from space, which collide with atoms in the atmosphere high above the Earth and make them glow. The eerie spectacle is seen regularly in the northern latitudes but has often been misinterpreted on its occasional appearances farther south. It may have been responsible for some of the stories of angelic hosts and ghostly armies seen in the sky. Seen low over the horizon, the aurora can look like lights on the ground in the distance, and could have given rise to stories of ghostly activity

along the shores of Long Island that believe there is a regular phantom craft that comes in on and off – sort of a coaster in the spirit trade.'

This belief was first investigated in some depth by Professor W. F. Ganong at the turn of the century and his findings were published by the *Bulletin* of the National Historical Society of New Brunswick. After interviewing numerous witnesses and examining all the evidence, he made four positive points on what he called 'The fact basis of the fire (or phantom) ship':

> It appears to the author plain that (1) a physical light is frequently seen over the waters, (2) that it appears at all seasons, or at least in winter and summer, (3) that it usually precedes a storm, (4) that its actual form is roughly hemispherical with the flat side to the water, and that at times it simply glows without much change of form, but that at other times it rises into slender moving columns, giving rise to an appearance capable of interpretation as the flaming rigging of a ship.

Professor Ganong inclined to the opinion that the 'phantom' was due to St Elmo's fire, but cautiously added that he was 'not aware of any reports of similar phenomena, of such frequency in one locality, and of such considerable development.'

Only a decade afterwards, however, very similar spook lights were the subject of a Government enquiry. Since about 1850 the people of the Rattlesnake Knob area of North Carolina had observed lights, sometimes red, sometimes yellowish white, appearing over the 2500-foot (760-metre) plateau of Brown Mountain, a blunt outcrop of the Appalachians. Stories grew of spirits on the mountain, though some citizens went in search of brush fires – to no avail.

The Brown Mountain lights continued to be seen for over 60 years, until finally a North Carolina Congressman mentioned the curiosity in Washington, and in 1913 an investigator from the United States Geological Survey was sent down to view it. Examining the mountain, he found that it consisted of ordinary Cranberry granite, which is widespread in the area. There was no marshland on the mountain's slopes, so the 'will o' the wisp' theory was ruled out. Witnesses said that the lights usually appeared at about seven in the evening, stayed for about 30 seconds, and then vanished, often to reappear 'four or five times' before dying out for the night. Others reported a single light that rose from the slopes of the mountain, hovered and then disappeared 'like a bursting skyrocket'.

Investigation renewed

The geologist was perfunctory in his report, ascribing all the lights to locomotive headlights. The Congressman who had instigated the enquiry in the first place was annoyed, and insisted that a second man be sent. The new investigator was more thorough but, after studying maps and geological details of the area, claimed that 47 per cent of the phenomena originated in locomotive headlights, 33 per cent in those of cars, and the remaining 20 per cent in fixed lights and bush fires equally. He added that the countryside at the foot of Brown Mountain was alternately dusty and misty, a combination of conditions that made the air very refractive.

However, a further report in 1925 pointed out several fairly obvious faults in the refraction theory, not the least of which was that the lights had been faithfully recorded for over 70 years – several decades before railroads were built in the area and half a century before the first automobile made its appearance. Furthermore, a season of floods in 1916 had put both railroads and highways out of action for some time, and still the 'phantom' lights appeared. One perhaps significant pointer was given: the lights disappear for long stretches during and for some time after a protracted drought. It may be that water – either the ocean or a river – is in cases such as this conducive to the appearance of ghost lights. (The John River runs by Brown Mountain.) Since 1925, no one has offered any further explanation – but the lights shine on.

In the 'tri-state' area where Kansas, Missouri and Oklahoma meet, spook lights appear so regularly that they have become a tourist industry. This area forms a triangle, the points of which are the towns of Columbus, Joplin, and Miami, about 20 miles (30 kilometres) from each other. Again a river, the Spring, cuts through this triangle, and the nearby US Highway 66 has given rise to the theory that the lights are those of automobiles, refracted by mist rising from the river. In favour of this is that fact that, viewed through binoculars, some of the lights appear in parallel pairs, with both members of each pair either white or red – like the head and tail lights of cars on a motorway.

Against the theory is the objection posed at Brown Mountain – that the lights have a venerable history dating far back beyond the automobile. And, like those of Ada, they occasionally bound up to onlookers; one farmer, ploughing by lamplight, abandoned his tractor and fled in terror when a red globe zoomed at him. So far, however, the lights have done no more than frighten and fascinate – so much so that for the past decade the hoteliers and bar-owners of the three towns have advertised the attractions of 'Spooksville', as they call it, in tourist brochures that they have distributed throughout the country.

Below: the proprietor of 'Spookers' Shanty', near Joplin, Missouri, has managed to make a profit out of the local mystery lights. The lights are visible here beyond the bushes. As the sign indicates, the Moon and planets are alternative attractions when the spook lights do not appear

Bottom: a group of the Joplin spook lights in the far distance, captured in a prize-winning photograph. Spook lights at other locations appear in conditions remarkably similar to these: down tree-lined highways or along railway tracks

There are a number of other 'spook light' sites in the United States. One of the best documented and most intriguing must be that on a hill in the Wet Mountain Valley area of Colorado, not only because the lights have appeared almost every night for just over 100 years, but also because they focus on that favourite scene of traditional hauntings – a disused cemetery.

In 1880, the township of Silver Cliff grew up in the wake of a sudden 'silver rush' and by the end of its first year's existence the population topped 5000. Due to the usual deaths by violence and mining incidents, a 'Boot Hill' cemetery grew at the same time on the foothills of Wet Mountain. The boom faded as quickly as it came, however, and today only about 100 prospectors live among the dilapidated buildings.

The strange phenomena that haunt the Silver Cliff graveyard were first reported shortly after its foundation, when a group of drunken miners returning to their diggings reported seeing eerie blue lights hovering over each grave. Nor were these lights just a by-product of whiskey – they appeared on other nights to sober observers. In 1956 an article about the lights in the *Wet Mountain Tribune* excited some comment in the Western United States, but it was not until 1967 that the *New York Times* sent a reporter to Silver Cliff to make an investigation.

Two years later, in an article about Colorado in the *National Geographic*, assistant editor Edward J. Linehan described how he viewed the lights in the company of Westcliffe resident Bill Kleine. It was dark when the two reached the graveyard, and Linehan switched off his headlights. They got out of the car, and Kleine pointed: 'There! See them? And over there!'

Linehan saw them, '. . . dim round spots of blue white light' glowing above each grave. He stepped forward for a better look at one but it vanished, then slowly reappeared. He switched on his flashlight and aimed it at one of the lights. The beam revealed only a headstone. For 15 minutes the men pursued the elusive ghost lights among the graves.

Most people, said Kleine, reckoned that the lights were 'reflections' of the town lights of Westcliffe. Looking back at the tiny cluster far below, Linehan found this impossible to believe, particularly as Kleine went on: 'Both me and my wife have seen them when the fog was so thick you couldn't see the town at all.'

Other theories recounted and discounted by Linehan were that the lights were caused by radioactive ore – but a Geiger counter test of the whole area revealed no trace of radioactivity; that the ghost lights were luminous paint, daubed on the tombs by hoaxers – but no evidence has ever been found to support this charge. Gas from decaying bodies seemed a far-fetched idea, as the last burial took place around the turn of the century. The mercury vapour lights of Westcliffe might, it was suggested, have caused 'special effects' on the hill side; but not only were they a late installation but on several occasions when power cuts had blacked out every township for miles around, the graveyard illuminations still shone.

Among the old-timers of Silver Cliff only one explanation holds good, said Linehan: the blue-white spots are the helmet lamps of long-dead miners, still seeking on the deserted hillside for traces of silver.

The curse on Killakee

From the days of the Dublin Hell Fire Club to the times of the Troubles, the history of Killakee House was stained by violence and bloodshed. This chapter tells the story of a disturbed past and its modern legacy: hauntings by a frightening supernatural beast

THE VICTORIAN WRITER E. Bulwer-Lytton used the phrase *Haunters and haunted* as a title for a celebrated story. He implied by the phrase that there was a definite relationship between the phenomena witnessed at a haunted house and the people who witnessed them – it was not a matter of chance that one person should see a ghost while another did not do so.

This certainly seems to be true in many well-attested poltergeist cases. These disturbances frequently centre on adolescents, and several researchers go so far as to claim that in such cases the 'haunters' emanate from the minds of the 'haunted' themselves, and are simply physical manifestations of teenage traumas. In other cases the person most closely involved in the phenomena appears to act as a catalyst for an already well-established haunting, fanning its embers into flame by his mere presence.

A combination of these factors may have been present when Killakee House in County Dublin became the centre of a veritable storm of psychic activity in the late 1960s and early 1970s. The onset of the phenomena occurred when new residents moved in, and ended when they left.

A story by Edward Bulwer-Lytton (below) suggests that hauntings can be caused by their 'victims'. Did something like this happen at Killakee House?

Killakee lies in the foothills of the Wicklow Mountains, overlooking the city of Dublin. Killakee House, built in the early 18th century as the dower house of the Massey family, is a robust stone building with a small tower. Behind the house rises the steep slope of Montpellier Hill, its scrubby grass worn bare by the feet of tourists hardy enough to make the ascent to the top. On the summit stands the stone shell of a fire-ravaged hunting lodge, constructed by the Earl of Rosse in the 18th century. It was used by him and such 'bucks' as Harry Barry, first Lord Santry, and Richard 'Burnchapel' Whaley as the headquarters of the Dublin Hell Fire Club – a close imitation of the contemporary English version founded by Sir Francis Dashwood.

Rosse had a cruel sense of humour and a hatred of black cats. He used to hold court at the Eagle Tavern on Cork Hill in Dublin. On one occasion, to frighten the local inhabitants, he doused a black cat in spirits, set it alight and watched it run screaming down the hill. Dubliners swore that it was the Devil himself.

There is strong evidence that Rosse's brutal and puerile humour was given play at the hunting lodge on Montpellier Hill. On one occasion, after a black mass, he put a black cat in the seat of honour when Satan failed to turn up in person. It was also said that a half-witted dwarf with a twisted body and unnaturally large head was beaten to death by Rosse and his cronies, shortly before the lodge burned down in the 1750s.

Rosse's friends often lodged with him in Killakee House and violent scenes often took place there. The Irish rakes were addicted to pistol duelling (one of the first questions asked by a prospective father-in-law of a noble suitor was 'do you blaze?', meaning 'do you fight duels?'). At least three deaths from duelling took place in the grounds.

Violence renewed

After a long interval that was relatively untroubled, there was again bloodshed at the house in the early 20th century. The house was then occupied by Countess Constance Markievicz, the 'Red Countess'. A friend of the mystical poet William Butler Yeats, she was the first woman to be elected to the House of Commons, although she never took her seat. The Countess participated in the 1916 rebellion, and five IRA men died in a gun battle at the house during her tenancy. All in all, Killakee House and the surrounding area were imbued with more violence and savagery than most haunted places.

Killakee House lay empty and derelict for some years after the Second World War. In the late 1960s it was bought by Mrs Margaret O'Brien, who wanted a centre in which Irish artists and sculptors could work and exhibit their art. When she moved into the place in 1968, she heard stories from locals that its grounds were haunted by a black cat the size of an Airedale dog. 'Haunted' was an appropriate term because the stories covered a period of over 50 years – much longer than the life-span of a normal cat.

Mrs O'Brien knew some of the tales related about her new property and its environs, and was rather shaken when she caught glimpses of a 'big black animal' disappearing into the thick shrubbery of her garden. She thought no more about it, however, until her friend Tom McAssey, a Dublin artist, and two colleagues had a terrifying experience one night while redecorating Killakee House in March 1968. They were working on the stone-flagged front hall, which opened onto what had been a ballroom. McAssey told a radio reporter:

> I had just locked the heavy front door, pushing a 6-inch [15-centimetre] bolt into its socket. Suddenly one of the two men with me said that the door had opened again. We turned, startled. The lock was good and the bolt was strong, and both fastened on the inside.
>
> We peered into the shadowed hallway, and then I walked forward, and sure enough the door stood wide open, letting in a cold breeze. Outside in the darkness I could just discern a black-draped figure, but could not see its face. I thought someone was playing a trick

Left: Tom McAssey's painting of the Black Cat of Killakee, which scared him and two companions one night in 1968. The picture now hangs in the house, which is an art centre

Below: the long low bulk of Killakee House stands beneath the hill on which the burnt-out ruin of the Hell Fire Club stands. A prehistoric cairn and a standing stone existed on the hill's summit before these buildings were put up

and said: 'Come in. I see you.' A low, guttural voice answered: 'You can't see me. Leave this door open.'

The men standing behind me both heard the voice, but thought it spoke in a foreign language. They ran. A long-drawn-out snore came from the shadow, and in panic I slammed the heavy door and ran too. Halfway across the gallery I turned and looked back. The door was again open and a monstrous black cat crouched in the hall, its red-flecked amber eyes fixed on me.

Beside Killakee House in a trailer in the wooded grounds lived Val McGann, a former Irish pole-vault champion who painted and showed his work at the gallery. He evinced no surprise at McAssey's story, because he had seen the huge cat on several occasions, lurking in the scraggling undergrowth of the overgrown garden.

'The first time I saw it, it frightened me stiff,' he said, 'but on subsequent occasions I have been more interested and amazed at the size of the beast. It is about the size of a biggish dog, with terrible eyes. I've even stalked it with my shotgun, but have never been able to corner it.'

For some months after McAssey's vision, apparitions were seen by workmen and artists at Killakee. They usually appeared at night, although two men saw what they thought was a nun, with her back to them, at midday in the old ballroom. When they approached her she disappeared, and a subsequent search of the house and garden failed to turn up any evidence of a real figure.

Following reports in the Dublin press and on television of the strange hauntings, a group of Irish show-business personalities persuaded Mrs O'Brien to let them try a seance in Killakee House. They included a stage conjurer who was an expert on illusions and who believed that he could rule out any 'fakery' on the part of residents.

The group arranged cards carrying the letters of the alphabet in a circle on a table and placed an upturned glass in the centre. Each participant rested one finger lightly on the glass. Those who have tried this well-known technique will know that the glass will slide around the table, from letter to letter, apparently spontaneously, with no one present applying any pressure to it – consciously, at any rate.

The group at Killakee asked any 'spirits' present to manifest themselves – but the 'replies' were gibberish. However, on two occasions the lights failed, although a subsequent check of the fuses revealed no fault, and the light bulbs and wiring appeared to be completely normal.

Two days later, however, events began to take a more frightening turn. First there were bumps and knockings in the night. Lights were switched rapidly on and off.

Bells in the night

Throughout the whole of one night the sound of door bells, in the front and back halls, could be heard. Yet those bells had been removed many years before.

A minor but curious manifestation was the fact that none of the residents – five or six in all – was able to sleep even on 'calm' nights; after retiring to bed exhausted from a heavy day's work, they reported lying awake, tossing and turning and managing to sleep only after sunrise.

About four days after the seance, everyone in the house heard heavy crashes and went to investigate. They found large pieces of furniture – some stored in locked rooms – thrown 'like matchboxes', some upside down, some pushed into corners. One oak medieval chair had been carefully pulled apart, joint from joint; even the brass tacks holding its tapestry in place had been pulled out and placed in neat rows. On the other hand, another similar chair had been smashed into tiny slivers.

After this outbreak, peace descended again for a matter of weeks. Then the 'haunters' turned their attention to exhibits on show in the house: a potter's works were hurled all over the room and smashed, while oil paintings were torn into long narrow strips.

At this point Margaret O'Brien sought the assistance of a priest, who, after obtaining permission from his superiors, performed a Roman Catholic rite of exorcism on Killakee House. The violent outbreaks stopped, but even more bizarre incidents began to occur in their place.

Mrs O'Brien had still not completed furnishing her house, and she lacked a refrigerator. She had asked the milkman to leave the milk in a pool in a cool stream that ran

Left: Countess Markievicz, who occupied Killakee House for a period. She was sentenced to death for her part in the 1916 uprising, but this was commuted to penal servitude for life. She was actually released in 1917 and became a noted Irish politician

Below: the building used by the Hell Fire Club as it was at the height of the society's infamy. It was built about 1725 as a hunting lodge, and commanded magnificent views of the mountains and forests of the surrounding countryside. It was burned down in mysterious circumstances – supposedly during one of the club's orgies of violence

Above: duelling, then a legal activity, claimed the lives of several noblemen at Killakee House during the 18th century. A duel could be substituted for a trial: the defendant had the right to challenge his accuser. Even after the abolition of such 'judicial' duels, personal combat, regulated by strict rules, remained legal between military men until it was finally outlawed in the mid 19th century

through the grounds. After the exorcism, Mrs O'Brien found that all the tinfoil tops had been removed from the bottles, although the milk was undisturbed.

Furthermore, no trace of the foil could be found. Mrs O'Brien assumed that it had been carried off by birds, possibly magpies or jackdaws. To stop the nuisance, she had a heavy four-sided box of stone built in the stream, with a large slate lid. Nevertheless, the caps continued to disappear.

The humour of the haunters

At this juncture, the 'haunters' showed a trace of humour as well as causing a rare psychic manifestation called an 'apport' – the sudden appearance of objects through apparently preternatural means. Following the disappearance of the caps from the bottles, 'caps' began to appear in the house itself – but these caps were types of headgear.

After the manifestations, Mrs O'Brien had made a practice of locking and checking all the doors before retiring. Despite this, a profusion of small caps began to appear all over the house. They would appear in odd places – on picture hooks or behind doors. Sometimes, rosary beads would be found, equally inexplicably.

At the end of 1970 the caps ceased to appear, although spasmodic knockings in the night continued to be heard. Then, a few months later, came a discovery that might have had a grim bearing on the whole strange series of incidents. While structural alterations to the kitchen were being made, an excavation for new plumbing was carried out. In a shallow grave a few feet under the surface was found the skeleton of a dwarf, with a skull too large for its small frame – a sinister echo of the legend told of the Hell Fire Club for so many years. In the grave, too, was a brass figurine, depicting a horned and tailed devil thumbing its nose.

Once again the priest was called, this time to conduct a proper burial service on the unknown unfortunate, and after that the manifestations ceased. Mrs O'Brien sold the premises six years later.

Was the Black Cat of Killakee – later portrayed in oils by Tom McAssey as he had seen it on that frightening night – a manifestation that was attached to the house, or had it somehow been conjured into existence by the new occupants? Were the voices, the bells and the broken furniture results of the seance, which somehow provided a focus for them? Or was the whole series of hauntings provoked by the unhappy ghost of the dwarf, brutally murdered, according to legend, by the drunken bucks of the Hell Fire Club?

It is unlikely that the answer will ever be known for sure, but we do know that all psychical phenomena ceased in 1977, when Joseph Frei took over the unfortunate house and added a restaurant to the art centre's facilities.

'Perhaps the previous owners were, shall we say, unlucky with the place,' he said. 'I and my family have been very happy here – I know about the history of it, but we have only experienced a feeling of warmth and comfort. Perhaps the "haunters" like what we are doing with their "haunt".'

The horror of Glamis

For centuries Glamis Castle has had a reputation as a place of strange and awful happenings – events that strike terror at the hearts of all who witness them. So what truth lies behind this ancient haunting?

GLAMIS CASTLE stands in the great vale of Strathmore in Tayside, Scotland. For hundreds of years the vast fortified house with its battlements and pointed towers – looking like the setting for a fairy tale – has been the ancestral home of the Earls of Strathmore. Their family secret is reputedly hidden within the walls of Glamis, famous as one of the most haunted houses on earth.

That there was unpleasantness within the castle's walls is an undoubted historical fact. And that the castle is today the centre of a triangle formed by three biblically named villages – Jericho, Zoar, and Pandanaram – may indicate the terror felt by its minions, for, according to a Scottish National Trust guidebook, the men who built and named them 'had at least some knowledge of the Scriptures and regard for the wrath of God'. That wrath, claim locals even today, was called down on Glamis for the sins of the first dozen or so Lairds. The present, 17th Earl of Strathmore, Fergus Michael Claude Bowes-Lyon, is well-liked by his tenants, and there is no evidence that his immediate forbears

Below: Glamis Castle, picturesque home of the Earl of Strathmore and Kinghorne, was a wedding gift from King Robert II upon the marriage of his daughter to Sir John Lyon in the 14th century. From the time Sir John moved to Glamis, the family seemed to be dogged by misfortune

Right: the painting of the third Earl, Patrick, with his children and greyhounds dominates the far wall of the drawing room at Glamis. It is around Patrick that two of the strangest stories revolve

Above: Malcolm II, who reigned as King of Scotland from 1005 until his death at Glamis in 1034 at the hands of an army of rebels. Tradition holds that he was slain in what is now known as King Malcolm's Room (top right), and that his brutal murder saw the start of the 'horror' at the castle

were any less affable; but the conduct of at least one of their ancestors called into being what is still known as the 'horror' of Glamis.

It is the nature of the horror that makes it one of the great mysteries. No recent Earl has ever spoken of it to an outsider, except in enigmatic terms. No woman has ever been let in on the secret. It is passed on only to the Strathmore heir on his 21st birthday.

The historical record of horror at Glamis Castle goes back to 1034, when King Malcolm II was cut down by a gang of rebellious subjects armed with claymores, the large broadswords peculiar to Scotland. It was said that every drop of Malcolm's blood seeped from his body into the floorboards, causing a stain that is still pointed out today, in what is called King Malcolm's Room. That the stain was made by Malcolm's blood is disputable, however, for records seem to show that the flooring has since been replaced. Nevertheless, Malcolm's killers added to the death toll of Glamis by trying to escape across a frozen loch, but the ice cracked and they were drowned.

Curse of the chalice

The Lyon family inherited Glamis from King Robert II, who gave it to his son-in-law, Sir John Lyon, in 1372. Until then the Lyon family home had been at Forteviot, where a great chalice, the family 'luck', was kept. Tradition held that if the chalice were removed from Forteviot House a curse would fall on the family; despite this, Sir John took the cup with him to Glamis. The curse seemed to have a time lapse, for though Sir John was killed in a duel, this did not occur until 1383; nevertheless, the family misfortunes are usually dated from this time.

The 'poisoned' chalice may well have influenced events 150 years later when James V had Janet Douglas, Lady Glamis, burned at the stake in Edinburgh on a charge of witchcraft. The castle reverted to the Crown, but after the falsity of the charge was proved, it was restored to her son. The spectre of Lady Glamis – the 'Grey Lady' as she is known – is said to walk the long corridors even today.

It was Patrick, the third Earl of Strathmore, who made the idea of a Glamis 'curse' widespread in the late 17th century; indeed, to many people he seemed the very embodiment of it. A notorious rake and gambler, his drunken debauches were well-known in London and Edinburgh as well as throughout his home territory. The facts of his career and his character are festooned with folklore, but he must have been something of an enigma, for despite his wild ways he was philanthropic towards his tenants at least. The Glamis Book of Record, for instance, details his plans for building a group of lodges on the estate for the use of retired workers. Now known as Kirkwynd Cottages, they were given to the Scottish National Trust by the 16th Earl of Strathmore in 1957 to house the Angus Folk Collection.

Two principal stories endure about Patrick. The first is that he was the father of a deformed child who was kept hidden somewhere in the castle, out of sight of prying eyes. The second is that he played cards with the Devil for his soul – and lost.

The first is fed by a picture of the third Earl that now hangs in the drawing room. It shows Patrick seated, wearing a classical bronze breastplate, and pointing with his left hand towards a distant, romanticised vista of Glamis. Standing at his left knee is a small, strange-looking green-clad child; to the child's left is an upright young man in scarlet doublet and hose. The three main figures are placed centrally, but two greyhounds in the picture are shown staring steadfastly at a figure, positioned at the Earl's right elbow. Like the Earl this figure wears a classical breastplate apparently shaped to the muscles of the torso – but if it is a human torso it is definitely deformed. The left arm is strangely foreshortened. Did the artist paint from life – and if so does the picture show the real horror of Glamis?

The second story goes like this. Patrick and his friend the Earl of Crawford were playing cards together one Saturday night. A servant reminded them that the Sabbath was approaching, to which Patrick replied that he would play on, Sabbath or no Sabbath, and that the Devil himself might join them for a hand if he so wished. At midnight, accompanied by a roll of thunder, the Devil appeared and told the card-playing Earls that they had forfeited their souls and were doomed to play cards in that room until Judgement Day.

The pact presumably came into operation only after Patrick's death, for there is some evidence that he revelled in the tale: but did he tell it merely as a joke or as some sort of elaborate cover up, to scare intruders forever from the castle? If the latter was his intention, it was strikingly successful. In 1957 a servant at the castle, Florence Foster, complained in a newspaper article that she had heard the Earls at their play in the dead of night, 'rattling dice, stamping and swearing. Often I lay in bed and shook with fright,' she said. She resigned rather than risk hearing the phantom gamblers again. The story persists of a 'secret room' known only to the Earls themselves, and it is true that no one knows for certain which of the hundred-odd rooms at Glamis was used by Patrick for his diabolical game of cards.

Grisly tales

One story tells – with curious precision – of a grey-bearded man, shackled and left to starve in 1486. A later one, which probably dates from before Patrick's time also, is gruesome in the extreme. A party of Ogilvies from a neighbouring district came to Glamis and begged protection from their enemies the Lindsays, who were pursuing them. The Earl of Strathmore led them into a chamber deep in the castle and left them there to starve. Unlike the unfortunate grey-bearded man, however, they had each other to eat and began to turn cannibal, some, according to legend, even gnawing the flesh from their own arms.

One or other of these tales may account for the ghost of a skeletally thin spectre known as Jack the Runner. And the ghost of a Negro pageboy, also seen in the castle, would seem to date from the 17th or 18th century, when young slaves were imported from the West Indies. A 'white' lady haunts the castle clock tower, while the grey-bearded man of 1486 appeared, at least once, to two guests simultaneously, one of whom was Mrs MacLagan, wife of the Archbishop of York at the turn of the 20th century. Mrs MacLagan told how, during her stay at the castle, one of the guests came down to breakfast and mentioned casually that she had been awakened by the banging and hammering of carpenters at 4 a.m. A brief silence followed her remarks, and then Lord Strathmore spoke and assured her that there were no workmen in the castle. According to another story, as a young girl Queen Elizabeth the Queen Mother (daughter of the 14th Earl, Claude George Bowes-Lyon) once had to move out of the Blue Room because her sleep was being disturbed by rappings, thumps, and footsteps.

Fascinating as all these run-of-the-mill ghosts and their distinguished observers are, however, it is the horror that remains the great mystery of Glamis. All the principal rumours – cannibal Ogilvies notwithstanding – involve a deformed child born to the

Below: Lady Elizabeth Bowes-Lyon, the future Queen Mother, grew up at Glamis. She is said to have felt the presence of the horror in the Blue Room

The 13th Earl of Strathmore, Claude Bowes-Lyon (left), was deeply troubled by the tales of strange events at Glamis. The wife of the Archbishop of York wrote that 'for many years, after the revelation of the secret, Claude was quite a changed man, silent and moody, with an anxious scared look on his face. So evident was the effect on him that his son, Glamis, when he came of age in 1876, absolutely refused to be enlightened'

The 14th Earl (below) and Mr Gavin Ralston, the estate factor (below right). When told the secret by the Earl, Mr Ralston was so appalled he vowed never to sleep at the castle again

family and kept in a secret chamber who lived, according to 19th-century versions of the story, to a preternaturally old age. In view of the portrait openly displayed in the Glamis drawing room, and always supposing that the mysterious child is actually portrayed, the subsequent secrecy seems rather pointless. If Patrick himself was prepared to have his 'secret' portrayed in oils, why should his successors have discouraged open discussion of the matter?

An unmentionable horror

Despite the secrecy, at the turn of the 19th century the stories were still flying thick and fast. Claude Bowes-Lyon, the 13th Earl who died in 1904 in his 80th year, seems to have been positively obsessed by the horror, and it is around him that most of the 19th-century stories revolved. It was he, for instance, who told an inquisitive friend: 'If you could guess the nature of the secret, you would go down on your knees and thank God it were not yours.' Claude, too, it was who paid the passage of a workman and his family to Australia, after the workman had inadvertently stumbled upon a 'secret room' at Glamis and been overcome with horror. Claude questioned him, swore the man to secrecy, and bundled him off to the colonies shortly afterwards. To a great extent the obsession seems to have visited itself upon his son, Claude George, the 14th Earl, who died in 1944.

In the 1920s, a party of 'gay young things' staying at Glamis decided to track down the 'secret chamber' by hanging a piece of linen out of every window they could find. When they finished they saw there were several windows they had not been able to locate. When the Earl learned what they had done he flew into an uncharacteristic fury. Unlike his forbears, however, Claude George broke the embargo on the secret by telling it to his estate factor, Mr Gavin Ralston, who subsequently refused to stay overnight at the castle again.

When the 14th Earl's daughter-in-law, the next Lady Strathmore, asked Ralston the secret, Ralston is said to have replied: 'It is lucky that you do not know and can never know it, for if you did you would not be a happy woman.'

That statement, surely, is the clue to the horror of Glamis. Old Patrick's deformed offspring did not alarm the father because nothing like it had been seen in the family before. Possibly the 'wicked' Earl rather delighted in him. But if the same deformity appeared even once in a later generation, the head of an ancient, noble and hereditary house would certainly have been reluctant to broadcast the fact. Perhaps Claude, 13th Earl of Strathmore, knew of such a second, deformed child in the Bowes-Lyon line, and passed the secret and the fear of its recurrence on to his successors?

Left: the chapel at Glamis where a secret room was discovered in the late 19th century. A workman came upon the door by chance and, finding that it led into a long passage, decided to investigate – but he emerged soon after, shaking with fright. He reported his experience to the Earl who, anxious to preserve the family secret, persuaded the man to emigrate

Mayfair's haunted house

For decades the elegant house in the heart of London's West End was plagued by ghosts, but each haunting seemed to take a new and different form. Experts may now have some explanations

IN 1884 the *National Observer* magazine published a poem by Rudyard Kipling. Entitled *Tomlinson*, it told the story of a London society 'waster' whose soul was rejected by the Devil on the grounds of mediocrity. But it was the setting of the poem that was calculated to interest the general public. It began:

Now Tomlinson gave up the ghost in
his house in Berkeley Square,
And a spirit came to his bedside and
gripped him by the hair . . .

For the previous four decades, Berkeley Square had been synonymous with ghosts (as it was with nightingales 60 years later).

According to popular rumour the focus of the trouble was No 50, a four-storey town house of brick and stone, built in the mid 18th century. For some years it had been the London home of Prime Minister George Canning (1770–1827), but it seemed unlikely that the supernatural disturbances in the house had any connection with his restless spirit. Canning was not particularly ethereal in life and in any case had breathed his last at Chiswick, some miles away.

The general consensus seemed to be that the 'thing' that haunted No 50 was 'too horrible to describe' – it seemed to be more a demon or terrible elemental than an ordinary ghost. Even before Bulwer Lytton used the house as a setting for his famous ghost story *The haunters and the haunted*, stories abounded of a 'nameless, slimy thing' that slithered up and down the stairs, leaving a foul-smelling, snail-like trail in its wake.

One tale, not unlike Bulwer Lytton's, told of two sailors who had broken into the empty house to shelter for the night. On the morrow, one was found dead, impaled on the railings in the street below, having leapt from the top storey in a frenzy of fear, while his companion was discovered white-haired and mad in the house itself.

No matter that no documentary evidence for such a remarkable incident existed. The story was firmly believed by society dandies and East End costermongers alike, and for several decades was kept alive by poems, newspapers and music hall songs.

Charles Harper, writing in 1907, remarked that 'the famous "haunted house" in Berkeley Square was long one of those things that no country cousin coming up from the provinces to London on sightseeing bent ever willingly missed.'

Harry Price investigated the mystery in the 1920s, two decades before his mishandling – or worse – of the Borley Rectory case made him an object of suspicion in psychical research circles. In the Berkeley Square investigation he seems to have done a

Above: 50 Berkeley Square as it appears today

Right: the front door, from behind which startled neighbours heard curious thumps, bumps and the ringing of bells

reasonably objective job: without, however, reaching any firm conclusions. On the one hand, he said, he had discovered some evidence that in the late 18th century – presumably before Prime Minister Canning's tenancy – the house had been the headquarters of a gang of forgers and coin clippers, who actively encouraged tales of the supernatural in order to disguise the true nature of the 'bumps in the night' that neighbours heard from time to time.

On the other hand he pointed out that the house had been empty for remarkably long periods and, while empty houses often tend to father ghost stories around themselves, 50 Berkeley Square was one of the most desirable addresses in London – so why had it been deserted for so long? Perhaps the rumours had some truth after all?

Left: Rudyard Kipling, from a portrait by Burne-Jones. Kipling's poem *Tomlinson* exploited the notoriety of the house in Berkeley Square – and helped sell out the magazine in which it appeared

Price's final surmise was that No 50 may well have been a target for poltergeist activity. In 1840, he discovered that several of the neighbours had heard a variety of noises coming from the empty premises, including bumps on the stairs, dragging noises as if heavy furniture were being moved about, tramping footsteps and, fairly regularly, the jangling of the signal bells below stairs.

One of the more headstrong neighbours, weary of the commotion, obtained a key and, as soon as he heard the bells tinkling, dashed into the house and down to the kitchen. He found the bells still bouncing on their curled springs, but no other sign of life in the locked house. All this, pointed out Price, fitted exactly with the type of phenomenon described by the Society for Psychical Research as poltergeist activity: the one difference being that poltergeists – in practically all known cases – centre themselves on people.

In the course of his investigation Price had had to wade through a great deal of speculative data that rarely gave dates or names. For instance, in the 1870s the magazine *Notes and Queries* had launched an investigation into the case, culminating in a long series by the writer W. E. Howlett.

> The mystery of Berkeley Square still remains a mystery [he wrote]. We are in hopes that during the last fortnight a full, final, and satisfactory answer would have been given to our questions: but we have been disappointed. The story of the haunted house in the heart of Mayfair can be recapitulated in a few words. . . . The house in Berkeley Square contains at least one room of which the atmosphere is supernaturally fatal to body and mind. A girl saw, heard, or felt such horror in it that she went mad, and never recovered sanity enough to tell how or why.
>
> A gentleman, a disbeliever in ghosts, dared to sleep in it and was found a corpse in the middle of the floor after frantically ringing for help in vain. Rumour suggests other cases of the same kind, all ending in death, madness or both as a result of sleeping, or trying to sleep in that room. The very party walls of the house, when touched, are found saturated with electric horror. It is uninhabited save by an elderly man and his wife who act as caretakers; but even these have no access to *the* room. This is kept locked, the key being in the hands of a mysterious and seemingly nameless person who comes to the house once every six months, locks up the elderly couple in the basement, and then unlocks *the* room and occupies himself in it for hours.

In 1881, an anonymous writer, again in *Notes and Queries*, testified to the truth of the

Right: Edward Bulwer Lytton, who used 50 Berkeley Square as a setting for a gruesome short story

'electric party walls' story, though he too failed to name names, possibly because the witnesses were 'society people'.

The incident in question had taken place at a ball given in 49 Berkeley Square early in the season of 1880. 'A lady and her partner,' said the writer, 'were sitting against the party wall of number fifty when on a sudden she moved from her place and looked around. The gentleman was just going to ask the reason when he felt impelled to do the same. On comparing their impressions, both had felt very cold and had fancied that someone was looking over their shoulders from the wall behind! From this it would appear that "stone walls do not a prison make" for these uncomfortable ghosts, who can project themselves right through them to the great discomfort of the next door neighbours.'

The most likely explanation of the origins of No 50's sinister reputation was printed shortly after this account appeared, and differed from most in that it could be verified, at least in part: doubtless because the parties mentioned were dead. According to the writer, in *Pall Mall* magazine, the house had been bought after George Canning's death by an Hon. Miss Curzon, who lived there from time to time until her death in 1859 at the age of 90. It was then leased by her executors to a Mr Myers, a well-to-do man about town who was engaged to be married and who spent the next few months of his tenancy redecorating and furnishing, only to have his bride jilt him on the eve of her wedding day. The unfortunate Myers became a recluse in his new home, developing a curiously Dickensian character, part Scrooge, part Miss Havisham.

In 1873 he was prosecuted by Westminster council for non-payment of rates, and refused to answer the summons in person. Despite this, the magistrate gave him time to pay, and was surprisingly lenient with him in his summing up: 'The house in question is known as "the haunted house" and has occasioned a good deal of speculation among the neighbours. Mr Myers' failure to pay his rates had arisen from eccentricity.'

The *Pall Mall* author went on: 'The disappointment [of his rejection] is said to have broken his heart and turned his brain. He became morose and solitary, and would never allow a woman to come near him. The miserable man locked himself away in the ill-fated top room of the house, only opening the door for meals to be brought to him occasionally by a manservant. Generally speaking he slept during the day and, at night, would emerge from his self-imposed exile to wander, candle in hand, around the house that was to have been the scene of his happiness.'

Possibly Myers was the 'mysterious and nameless person' alluded to by W. E. Howlett, for he died, apparently, towards the end of the 1870s.

'Thus,' said the writer in *Pall Mall*, 'upon the melancholy wanderings of this poor lunatic, was founded that story of the

Below: Berkeley Square in the 1860s. The macabre goings-on at No 50 sorted ill with its gentility and refinement

ghost . . . those whom so many persons insist on calling "mad doctors" could tell of hundreds of cases of minds diseased and conduct similar to that of poor Myers. His sister was, it was said, his only relative, and she was too old or great an invalid to interfere.'

New twists to the tale

There the story should have ended, but did not. In 1912, Jessie A. Middleton, a popular author on the occult, wrote in her *Grey ghost book* that her own research had shown that the ghost was that of a little girl in a Scots kilt. She claimed that the child had been either frightened or starved to death in the fourth-floor room and had been seen there from time to time ever since, weeping and wringing her hands in dismay. But Miss Middleton added that another version of the story – echoing the 'falling sailor' tale – held that the girl had not been so young, that her name was Adeline, and that rather than submit to a 'fate worse than death' at the hands of her wicked guardian, she had leapt from the window and been spiked to death on the area railings.

As late as 1969 another strand was added to the already tangled skein of the Berkeley Square affair. Mrs Mary Balfour, an octogenarian lady of noble Scottish family, whose letters from society names attested to her apparently remarkable powers of clairvoyance, told a reporter of the only actual ghost that she had seen. Early in 1937 she had moved with her maid into a flat in Charles Street, which is adjacent to Berkeley Square, having lived previously in the Highlands of Scotland.

'It was about the time of New Year,' she recalled, 'and I had come in late when my maid summoned me to the kitchen at the back of the flat. We could see into the back windows of a house diagonally opposite and in one of them stood a man in a silver-coloured coat and breeches of eighteenth-century cut, wearing a periwig and with a drawn, pale face. He was looking out sadly, not moving. I thought perhaps that he had been to some New Year party in fancy dress, and either had a hangover or some personal trouble, I rebuked the girl for staring at him so. It was only afterwards that I discovered that the house was number fifty. Believe it or not, I had not until that time heard of the reputation of the house.'

If Mrs Balfour had not, many people had, and stories about No 50 Berkeley Square continue to circulate even today. In the early years of the Second World War the house was taken over by antiquarian book sellers Maggs Brothers Ltd. According to a spokesman, in late 1981 they were still getting three or four calls a month from tourists seeking the ghosts: 'Unfortunately we can tell them nothing. The so-called "haunted room" is next to the accounts department; none of us has ever seen, or heard, or felt anything out of the ordinary there. During the war members of the staff used the room as a dormitory while firewatching without any discomfort apart from draughts. I can only regretfully suppose that the ghost was exorcised long before our arrival.'

Above: reputedly the seat of all the disturbances – the haunted room at No 50, now quiet and tranquil as part of a modern office

Left: George Canning, sometime Prime Minister, who owned – but apparently did not return to haunt – the house in Berkeley Square

The ghost and the gossips

The couple who took up lodgings at the home of Richard Parsons seemed ordinary enough. But with their arrival came a series of events that left Parsons fearing for his sanity – and his life

THE 18TH CENTURY, dubbed by the Victorians 'The Age of Reason', was in fact extravagantly credulous. In spite of – or perhaps because of – the influence of rationalists such as Rousseau and Voltaire, the great ruck of citizens, from high courtiers to low commoners, were obsessed with the supernatural, the unnatural and the downright bizarre.

Sir Isaac Newton, discoverer of gravity, President of the Royal Society and Master of the Royal Mint, spent the last quarter of a century before his death in 1727 in the study of alchemy. Ben Franklin, the writer John Wilkes and the satirical poet Charles Churchill donned monks' robes and cavorted at Sir Francis Dashwood's Hell Fire Club on the Thames, acting only half in jest. Nathanael St André, George I's resident anatomist, ruined his reputation by backing the claim of a woman named Mary Tofts, who swore that she had given birth to a litter of rabbits. And an oak tree in an inn yard near Winchester that groaned out prophecies attracted queues of stately carriages until a speaking tube was discovered leading from its trunk to the landlord's quarters.

More seriously, an 18-year-old servant girl named Elizabeth Canning disappeared for a month in 1753 and then reappeared to claim that she had been held captive in a brothel at Enfield, about 10 miles (15 kilometres) from her home in the City of London. She named her captive as Mother Wells, the 'madam', and her gypsy servant Mary Squires. They had, said Elizabeth, left her in a darkened room with only a loaf of dry bread and a jug of water for sustenance. Nevertheless 'angelic' intervention had kept her alive and fit enough to break out, at the end of the month, and walk home.

Despite the oddity of the story, the great Bow Street magistrate and novelist Henry Fielding believed it and sent Wells and Squires for trial at the Old Bailey. Wells was condemned to death, and Squires to branding and six months' hard labour. Fortunately, the Lord Major of London, Sir Crisp Gascoyne, had sufficient sense of the ridiculous to check the story further; he discovered incontrovertible evidence that the two accused had not been near Enfield at the time,

In the 18th century, it seems there were no limits to the extent of human credulity. For example, the claim made by Mary Tofts that she had given birth to a litter of rabbits (below) was apparently readily accepted by at least one eminent physician. And, in 1749, crowds of the curious crammed a London theatre to witness for themselves the amazing powers of the mysterious 'bottle conjurer', who – it was promised – would disappear into a wine bottle on stage and sing from inside it. He would also 'play' a common walking stick, reproducing the sound of any instrument then in use, and for an extra gratuity would raise the spirit of any historical character. The 'bottle conjurer' did indeed disappear, but before the performance – and along with the considerable box office takings

and they were released and pardoned – though not before pretty Mary Squires had been scarred with the branding iron.

The Canning affair had much in common with one of the greatest talking points of the century, the business of 'Scratching Fanny' – the ghost of Cock Lane. In both cases the credulous clamour of the mob put lives and reputations at stake on the flimsiest of evidence while eminent men looked on. Both cases promoted songs, poems, theatrical burlesques and controversy. But the hindsight of over two centuries and the light of modern psychical research suggest that something paranormal could have happened at Cock Lane, and that 18th-century mass hysteria may for once have clouded a real and striking case of poltergeist activity in the classic mould.

Cock Lane is a short, curving thoroughfare in the City of London on the fringes of Smithfield. In the mid 18th century it was a slightly run down, though respectable, area containing private houses, a tavern called the Wheat Sheaf, tradesmen's shops and a charity school. At what is now No 20 lived Richard Parsons, who drew a stipend as officiating clerk at the nearby church of St Sepulchre, Snow Hill, and had a wife and two young daughters, the eldest, Elizabeth, being about 11 years old when the Cock Lane mystery began.

Top: the modern Cock Lane, in the City of London. Situated on the outskirts of Smithfield (above), the street became the subject of gossip and scandal in the mid 18th century, for one of the houses was said to be haunted – by the ghost of a woman who seemed to be seeking revenge for her own untimely death

Today, Parsons would probably be considered a scandal to the church, for he was a heavy drinker with a tendency to run into debt, particularly with his accommodating friend James Franzen, landlord of the Wheat Sheaf. In 1759, however, his drinking habits were no better and no worse than those of many another minor cleric, and he kept himself solvent by taking in lodgers.

In October of that year, Parsons met a genteel looking couple who introduced themselves as Mr and Mrs William Kent, newly up from Norfolk and looking for lodgings until their house in Clerkenwell was ready for them. Parsons was happy to take them in, particularly because William Kent, after paying his rent in advance, lent Parsons 12 guineas, to be paid back at a guinea a month.

Soon landlord and lodger were on sufficiently friendly terms for William to let Parsons in on his secret: he and his 'wife' Frances, known as Fanny, were not married. Two years previously, William had kept an inn and a post office at the village of Stoke Ferry, Norfolk, and had married Elizabeth Lynes, the daughter of a well-to-do grocer. Unfortunately, Elizabeth was not strong and had a difficult pregnancy, during which her sister Fanny moved in with the Kents to look after her. Elizabeth died in childbirth, and her offspring died a month later. After going through this double tragedy together, William and Fanny had grown very close, but the law at the time forbade marriage between bereaved brothers- and sisters-in-law, so the pair had decided to live in sin. Coming up to London in the summer of 1759 they decided to prove their mutual love and trust by making wills in each other's favour. Fanny had the advantage here, for though, according to later testimony, she had 'a bare hundred pounds', William had 'a considerable fortune'. Apart from half a crown to each of her two brothers and four surviving sisters, Fanny left everything 'she had or might expect' to William 'at his absolute disposal'.

A disturbed relationship

The first intimation that something was odd about the house in Cock Lane came that autumn. Kent was out of town on business, and Fanny's maid, Esther Carlisle, a redhead nicknamed 'Carrots', had been given leave. Fanny was nervous about sleeping alone and asked Richard Parsons's elder daughter Elizabeth to share her four poster bed. During the few nights the pair slept together, both were awakened by a rapping noise, seemingly coming from the wainscot of the bedroom. Elizabeth asked her mother about the noise, and was told that it was probably made by the shoemaker next door, who was in the habit of working late. When the noise began on a Sunday night, however, the family became seriously alarmed, for the cobbler was absent; Parsons, the two women and Elizabeth all heard it.

The noise 'like knuckles rapping' went on night after night, and as the comfort of the household was disturbed, so was the relationship between William Kent and Richard Parsons. Parsons had failed to keep his agreement to repay a guinea a month to his lodger, and Kent, who by now was ready to move into his own house in Clerkenwell, put the matter into the hands of his attorney. The drunken Parsons rather spitefully reacted by broadcasting the news about the Kents' marital status, or lack of it, to all and sundry.

In January the Kents moved to Clerkenwell, but the pleasure of setting up home together was marred by the fact that Fanny,

The house in Cock Lane, home of the Parsons family, where every night strange rappings could be heard, apparently coming from the wooden panelling in one of the rooms. Despite investigation, no natural explanation of the sounds could be found – and Richard Parsons, the head of the household, began to fear that some supernatural agency was at work

six months pregnant, had become seriously ill. William hired a doctor and an apothecary to attend to her, and the doctor diagnosed 'a confluent smallpox of a very virulent nature'.

To the sanctimonious Parsons, Fanny's illness had been sent to 'punish her for her sins'. The knocking on his wainscot had not abated, and he was beginning to form a theory about that too: it was made by the ghost of Fanny's dead sister Elizabeth. His suspicions seemed confirmed when both he and James Franzen had a frightening experience towards the end of January.

Franzen had called at the house to see Parsons and, finding him out, had sat for a while with Mrs Parsons and her two daughters. The persistent knocking frightened him, however, and he got up to leave. As he reached the kitchen door 'he saw pass by him something in white, seemingly in a sheet, which shot by him and up stairs.' The vision gave off a radiance strong enough to illuminate the face of the clock in the charity school across the street.

Franzen, thoroughly alarmed, ran back to fortify himself with brandy at the Wheat Sheaf and had no sooner lifted the glass when he heard a thunderous knocking on his front door. When he had steeled himself to open it he found Parsons, white-faced and stammering on the doorstep.

'Give me the largest glass of brandy that you have,' demanded the cleric. 'Oh Franzen! As I was going into my house just now I saw the ghost.'

'And so did I!' replied the landlord. 'And have been greatly frightened ever since. Bless me! What can be the meaning of it? It is very unaccountable.'

Meanwhile there was alarm of a different kind in Clerkenwell, for Fanny Kent was dying. An acquaintance of William's, the Reverend Stephen Aldrich of St John's, Clerkenwell, and the doctor and apothecary sat with her night and day. In the last 50 hours of her life she could take nothing but a little liquid, prepared by the apothecary and administered by the doctor. On the evening of 2 February 1760, Fanny died.

William Kent was distraught with grief and ordered a decent coffin 'both lined and covered' but for fear of prosecution he asked the undertaker not to put a name plate on the lid; the risk was minimal, but nevertheless it was an offence to live together falsely as man and wife. Fanny was laid to rest in the 12th-century vaults of St John's, as her family fumed over the provisions in her will.

The rappings at Cock Lane continued; indeed, two new lodgers there, Catherine Friend and Joyce Weatheral, later testified that they had left the house rather than suffer them further. Frustrated and frightened, Parsons called in a carpenter, Bateman Griffiths, to strip away the wainscot to seek the cause of the trouble; nothing was found and the panelling was replaced. Then Parsons called in the Reverend John Moore, rector of St Bartholomew the Great, West Smithfield, to investigate the supernatural possibilities.

Poltergeist on trial

When investigators were called in to examine the 'ghost' of Cock Lane, they devised a test to establish once and for all who or what lay behind it. The revelations pointed to murder

Shops and taverns in the Cock Lane area did a roaring trade as a result of the activity at Richard Parsons's home, which daily drew crowds of sightseers to the street. Only the Parsons family, it seems, failed to profit from the phenomena

RICHARD PARSONS was becoming seriously alarmed by the mysterious noises at his home in Cock Lane. The strange rappings had continued for several months and no natural explanation could be found for them. Then, almost at his wits' end, Parsons asked the Reverend John Moore to investigate, to see if some paranormal agency were the cause.

Moore was a follower of John Wesley, who was himself no stranger to the supernatural. In 1715 Wesley's family home had been troubled by a 'knocking spirit', and his father, the Reverend Samuel Wesley, had 'communicated' with it by knocking back. Moore, told of Parsons's theories as to the origin of the phenomena – he now believed that the ghost of the newly dead Fanny Kent was responsible – began holding seances, using one knock for yes, and two for no, in order to find out the 'spirit's' wishes. The Wesley ghost had centred itself upon Hetty Wesley, John's younger sister, and the Cock Lane ghost now orientated itself upon the person of 11-year-old Elizabeth Parsons.

Moore's most productive sessions were held in Elizabeth's bedroom, after the girl had been put to bed. Sometimes the knocks came from the floorboards, sometimes from the bedstead or the walls. On the rare occasions when the 'spirit' appeared to be pleased, it made a noise like the fluttering of wings; when displeased it made a noise like 'a cat's claws scratching over a cane chair' – and it became known as 'Scratching Fanny'.

A demand for justice

Its message was brutally blunt. It was the ghost of Fanny Kent, murdered by William, who had poisoned her purl – a concoction of bitter herbs in ale popularly used as a restorative – about two hours before she died. Fanny wanted justice.

William Kent, slowly recovering from his bereavement, had set himself up as a stockbroker and busied himself in the City, and it was not until almost a year after Fanny's death, in January 1761, that he heard of the continuing saga of Cock Lane through a series of articles in the *Public Ledger* news sheet. Terrified by the 'ghost's' accusations – which were now, of course, public knowledge – he called on the Reverend Moore. Moore was impressed by Kent's manner and bearing, but assured him that 'there were very strange noises of knockings and scratchings every night, and that there was something behind darker than all the rest.'

As a result of their meeting, Kent went to Cock Lane to sit in on a seance himself. To his horror the knocks accused him personally of having killed Fanny with arsenic, and when he asked, at Moore's instigation, whether he would be hanged, the answer was a single knock.

'Thou art a lying spirit,' he shouted. 'Thou art not the ghost of my Fanny. She would never have said any such thing.'

By this time the ghost of 'Scratching

Fanny' had become a matter of enormous public interest, and crowds on foot and in carriages flocked to watch the comings and goings at the house. Horace Walpole wrote: 'Provisions are sent in like forage, and all the taverns and ale houses in the neighbourhood make fortunes.' To the credit of the Parsons family, however, none of them seems to have made any money from the phenomena.

As the year went on, so the seances continued. On one occasion, one of the sitters, William Legge, Earl of Dartmouth and himself a Methodist, decided to have Elizabeth Parsons moved to the house of a gentleman named Bray, just to see what would happen. The knockings accompanied her, seeming to show that she, and not the actual Cock Lane premises, was the catalyst. But the girl was watched closely, women attendants holding her hands and feet to rule out fraud, and still the noises went on.

The proceedings had taken on the atmosphere of a kangaroo court, with the doctor and apothecary who had attended Fanny Kent in her last illness denying that Kent could have poisoned her – she had drunk only their preparation in the 50 hours before her death – and the knocking contradicting them. The maid servant 'Carrots' Carlisle was implicated also, and indignantly shouted at the 'spirit': 'Then I am sure, Madam, you may be ashamed of yourself, for I never hurt you in my life.'

Elizabeth Parsons herself had begun to have epileptic fits. She claimed to have actually seen the ghost, 'in a shroud and without hands', but claimed that the only aspect of the matter that frightened her was 'what would become of her Daddy . . . if their matter should be supposed to be an imposture.'

William Kent was naturally anxious to clear up the matter; Moore, convinced that the ghost was telling the truth, was also eager for the authorities to act, but the only person in the City of London with the power to order a full investigation was the Lord Mayor, Sir Samuel Fludyer. He 'did not choose to stir much, for it was somewhat like Canning's affair', which had caused a great for his predecessor (see page 50), and he refused to order the arrest of either Kent – for suspected murder – or Parsons – for fraud. Instead, he insisted that an independent investigation should be held at the house of the Reverend Stephen Aldrich, vicar of St John's, Clerkenwell.

Above: Dr Samuel Johnson (left) with Oliver Goldsmith (centre). Johnson was one of the 'Committee of Gentlemen' formed by the vicar of St John's, Clerkenwell, and William Legge, Earl of Dartmouth (below), to investigate the Cock Lane affair and William Kent's role in it. The committee's findings – that no supernatural agency was involved – led to the publication of a pamphlet, generally believed to be the work of Oliver Goldsmith, which argued forcefully that Kent was innocent of all charges against him

Aldrich, to make sure that the investigation would be impartial, formed a committee with Lord Dartmouth. They chose Dr John Douglas, an amateur investigator who had exposed a number of frauds, Mrs Oakes, a hospital matron, Dr George Macaulay, a society physician, two or three gentlemen and Dr Samuel Johnson.

Johnson had long been fascinated by ghosts. The idea of total oblivion after death horrified him. He summed up his attitude to his biographer James Boswell: '. . . still it is undecided whether or not there has ever been an instance of the spirit of any person appearing after death. All argument is against it; but all belief is for it.'

But he undertook to assist in the investigation of 'Scratching Fanny' for a typically humanitarian reason. If the affair was a fraud, it was seriously damaging the reputation of William Kent, who seemed an honest and decent man.

The 'Committee of Gentlemen', as the newspapers termed it, decided on a new course of action. They arranged to test Elizabeth Parsons at Aldrich's house, and then, leaving her behind, they would descend to the vault of St John's, where the ghost would knock on Fanny Kent's coffin to 'prove' its objective existence. A preliminary seance was held, and the ghost agreed to these conditions.

The test begins

On the evening of 1 February 1762, Elizabeth was put to bed at Aldrich's house, attended by the matron, Mrs Oakes, and other women. According to Dr Johnson's report, the child said that she could feel the spirit 'like a mouse upon her back [but] no evidence of any preternatural power was exhibited'.

The committee then made its way to St John's, entered the vault, and called upon the spirit to keep its promise by knocking on the coffin. 'But nothing more than silence ensued. . . . It is therefore the opinion of the whole assembly that the child has some art of making or counterfeiting particular noises, and that there is no agency of a higher cause.'

One or two more seances followed, but the affair was nearing its end. On 3 February, a large gathering saw a curtain rod spin violently of its own volition, and heard a knocking of such violence, high up in the chimney, 'that they thought it would have broke it all to pieces'. Finally, Elizabeth was told that she had only one more night, 21 February, to prove her innocence, 'otherwise she and her

Above: St John's Church, Clerkenwell, where Fanny Kent was laid to rest in 1760. Although the investigating committee had, by implication, exonerated William Kent from the charge of Fanny's murder, the case was not closed. When the coffin was opened 90 years later, the corpse was found to be perfectly preserved – which, to modern forensic scientists, would suggest death by arsenic poisoning. So, was Fanny Kent murdered? And, if so, by whom? And why?

Left: John Wesley, whose family also experienced a 'knocking spirit', which centred on Wesley's younger sister – just as that at Cock Lane focused on 11-year-old Elizabeth Parsons. In the 18th century such disturbances were believed to be evil in nature; today they are recognised as classic symptoms of poltergeist activity

father and mother would all be sent to Newgate.'

This final session was held at the house of a gentleman named Missiter in Covent Garden and this time, perhaps not unexpectedly, there were positive results. The child was seen creeping from her bed to pick up a piece of wood with which she subsequently made knocking sounds. But Missiter and his companions agreed that this blatant piece of fraud produced sounds nothing like the ones heard previously: Elizabeth was, naturally, terrified for her freedom.

The tide had turned in Kent's favour. On 5 March a pamphlet entitled 'The mystery revealed', usually attributed to Oliver Goldsmith, put the case for his innocence with force. Later, Charles Churchill published a long poem, *The ghost*, which laughed at the affair – particularly Dr Johnson's part in it – and David Garrick turned the saga of 'Scratching Fanny' to good use by making it the centrepiece of a comic recitation, 'The Farmer's Return', at Drury Lane theatre.

On 9 February a new knocking ghost was advertised as 'likely to perform' in Broad Court, Covent Garden. The magistrate at nearby Bow Street was John Fielding, the half brother of Henry Fielding, and he sent the 'ghost' his compliments 'with an intimation that it would not meet with the lenity the Cock Lane spirit did, but that it should knock hemp in Bridewell. On which the ghost, very discreetly, omitted the intended exhibition.'

On 10 July, the 'conspirators' were brought for trial at the Court of King's Bench, Guildhall, before Lord Mansfield. The charge was that the Reverend John Moore, Richard Parsons, Mrs Parsons and others had conspired to 'take away the life of William Kent by charging him with the murder of Frances Lynes by giving her poison whereof she died'. James Franzen the landlord, 'Carrots' the servant, the doctor and the apothecary all gave evidence, while several people spoke up for Parsons.

After a trial lasting a day, the accused were found guilty. The Rev. Moore was heavily fined, Parsons was sentenced to two years' imprisonment and three sessions in the pillory, and his wife to one year's jail. Elizabeth Parsons did not stand trial, but was not, apparently, troubled by her 'ghost' again.

Even after leaving prison, Parsons protested his innocence, and his protests have a convincing ring to them. He had gained nothing from the Cock Lane affair but notoriety and punishment. He had had differences with Kent, it was true, but he was, drunkenness apart, a well-liked man of previous good character, with no wish to put another's life at stake. Furthermore hundreds of people – the Duke of York, Horace Walpole, and Lord Hertford included – had heard the knockings from the wainscot, a good distance from Elizabeth's bed.

A twist in the tale

And the manifestations themselves, centring on a young, prepubescent girl who had epileptic tendencies, closely echo modern cases held by parapsychologists to be 'genuine'. Perhaps the 'interpretation' of the Cock Lane rappings was the only fault of Parsons and Moore.

Or perhaps the 'ghost' had a point after all. The coffins were cleared from the vaults of St John's Church in 1860, but 10 years previously an illustrator, J. W. Archer, had visited them to produce illustrations for a book by Charles Mackay entitled *Memoirs of extraordinary popular delusions*, which featured the Cock Lane ghost. By the light of a lantern, the sexton's boy who accompanied Archer had opened the coffin said to be that of 'Scratching Fanny' and shown him the body within. The face was that of a once handsome woman, with a pronounced aquiline nose: 'an uncommon case,' wrote Archer, 'for the cartilage mostly gives way. The remains had become adipocere, and were perfectly preserved.'

There was no sign, as far as he could see, of the smallpox from which Fanny was said to have died. But the preservation of the features – the nose in particular – would unfailingly set a modern forensic scientist looking for traces of arsenic poisoning.

Burning with guilt

Left: Frendraught House, the family seat of the powerful Crichton clan for many years. Because of the tragedy that took place there in the 17th century, it is said to be haunted – and the wife of the present owner is one of the witnesses to the haunting

When a major feud between two great Scottish clans ended in a fire that killed several members of one faction, the local populace laid the blame on the lady of the manor. Today her guilt-ridden ghost still haunts the scene of the crime

ONE OF THE CLASSIC THEMES of supernatural lore is the unhappy ghost doomed to haunt the scene of its earthly wrongdoing until its sins are expiated. Is Frendraught House in Aberdeenshire just such a scene of a 'penitential' haunting? There are folklorists and witnesses who think that it is.

Frendraught House lies about 6 miles (9 kilometres) to the east of Huntly in the centre of the extensive Bognie estates. Its foundations date from 1203, though additions were made to it as recently as the 1840s. Its main bulk – containing inner walls up to 9 feet (2.7 metres) thick – was built between the 14th and 17th centuries when it was both home and fortress to the powerful Crichton family. During those three centuries the Crichtons, along with their cousins and neighbours the Gordons and Leslies, controlled the north-east of Scotland. They were often embroiled in bloody feuds.

In the spring of 1630 Frendraught was occupied by Sir James Crichton. He had made a good political marriage to Lady Elizabeth Gordon, eldest daughter of the Earl of Sutherland, and she took an active part in her husband's continual disputes. As one Victorian commentator put it, she played a role somewhere between that of Medusa and Lady Macbeth.

The 1630 dispute over boundary lands was between Sir James Crichton and Gordon, Laird of Rothiemay. Sir James settled it in typical fashion by shooting Gordon dead. The Marquis of Huntly, the local High Sheriff who was himself a Gordon closely related to both sides, fined Sir James heavily. This 'blood money' was paid to young John Gordon, the new Laird of Rothiemay, and honour seemed satisfied.

By midsummer, however, Sir James was fighting again, this time with Leslie of Pitcaple. Matters came to a head when a Crichton shot Leslie through the arm with an arrow. Again the Marquis of Huntly heard the case, this time ruling in favour of Sir James. The wounded Leslie rode off in a fury, openly swearing revenge on the house of Crichton. Sir James therefore took the precaution of assembling an armed party to escort him back to Frendraught. Surprisingly, it included young John Gordon of Rothiemay as well as the Marquis of Huntly's son, John Melgum Viscount Aboyne. The party arrived in the dusk of an October afternoon. Lady Crichton, perhaps relieved to see her husband home safe, pressed even the unloved Gordon kin to stay the night. The guests were put in the old tower.

Lord Melgum was given a room separated

Below: the scene of a modern-day haunting – part of the original old tower staircase at Frendraught. At the time of the fire, the rest of the tower staircases were wooden – and, burning fiercely, cut off the doomed guests

Right and below: Sir James and Lady Elizabeth Crichton. Their guests, among them some clan rivals, met death by fire at Frendraught House. Lady Crichton was known to be a strong support to Sir James in his many feuds, which may be why people thought her guilty of causing the fire

Below right: the Marquis of Huntly, the local High Sheriff, was closely involved in the events at Frendraught House – and not just as an official. His son, Lord Melgum, was one of those who burned to death in the old tower while trying to help the others

from the upper storeys by a wooden staircase. John Gordon of Rothiemay was on the second floor, and the other guests and servants above him. Spalding, a contemporary chronicler, tells what happened: 'About midnight that dolorous tower took fire in so sudden and furious a manner, and in ane clap, that the noble Viscount, the Laird of Rothiemay, English Will, Colonel Ivat and others, servants, were cruelly burned and tormented to death.'

Lord Melgum, it is said, ran to help the others, but the wooden stair caught fire and he was trapped with them. According to Spalding: 'They hurried to the window looking out into the close, piteously calling for help, but none was or could be rendered them.' Altogether about a dozen people lost their lives.

Death by design

An event of this magnitude cast shadows far beyond north-east Scotland, and the Privy Council in Edinburgh became involved, setting up a commission of bishops and neutral peers to investigate. The commission sat at Frendraught on 13 April 1631. The bishops merely declared that 'the fire could not have happened accidentally but designedly.' There the mystery of the fire rests, unsolved to this day. However, local opinion of the time laid the blame squarely on Lady Frendraught. An anonymous ballad written a few months after the event said of Rothiemay's final moments:

When he stood at the wire window
Most doleful to be seen
He did espy the Lady Frendraught
Who stood upon the green.
And mercy, mercy Lady Frendraught
Will ye not sink with sin
For first your husband kilt my father
And now ye burn his son.
Oh, then it spake Lady Frendraught
And loudly did she cry
It was great pity for good Lord John
But none for Rothiemay
But the keys are sunk in the deep
draw well
Ye cannot get away.

To the Marquis of Huntly there was only one way to avenge his dead son. Laying aside his High Sheriff's impartiality, he recruited a small army of highlanders and raided Frendraught, carrying off 60 cattle and several dozen sheep.

Crichton appealed to Edinburgh, and the Privy Council came down in his favour. Huntly was fined and Sir James received damages.

Despite their vindication by the Privy Council, both Sir James and his Lady seemed changed by the terrible fire. Three years afterwards he gave a silver chalice, said to have been one of 11 brought north by Mary Queen of Scots, to the nearby kirk at Forgue. Today the chalice, the oldest known

piece of hallmarked silver in Scotland, lies in a bank vault in Huntly.

Lady Frendraught took her three daughters and went to live as a recluse at Kinnairdy on the River Deveron. Born a Catholic, she was excommunicated when she signed the Solemn League and Covenant supporting Presbyterianism. Turning back to her old faith, she was rebuffed. 'I refused absolutely to see her,' wrote Father Blackhall, 'because

she was suspected to be guilty of the death of my Lord Aboyne. . . .' When she died, it was without benefit of clergy, on an unrecorded date. She was buried, like her husband, in an unmarked grave.

Sir James's eldest son was the last of his line. He was created Viscount Frendraught by his cousin Charles I for services rendered during the Civil War. After his death, his widow married George Morison of that Ilk, Chief of the Morison Clan and Laird of Bognie. His descendant, Alexander Gordon Morison, became Laird of Bognie and Mountblairy and owner of Frendraught House in 1942. He was born in Canada and inherited the chieftainship and family estates from his uncle. Immediately after the Second World War he and his young family lived at Frendraught House, but later moved to Mountblairy – not, he insists, for fear of ghosts, but for practical reasons. After several years of being leased, Frendraught House now stands empty.

'According to local opinion and the direct testimony of tenants, guests, and my wife,' says Mr Morison, 'Frendraught is haunted by Lady Elizabeth Crichton, who is bound there because of her guilt. I have never felt or seen anything myself, but according to legend the Laird never does anyway.' Mr Morison believes in Lady Crichton's guilt. He cites documents showing that, when the 'deep draw well' in the courtyard was cleaned out during alterations in the 1840s, massive keys were found. This supports the allegations of the old ballad.

The recorded sightings of a 'dark woman in a white dress' at Frendraught go back at least to the early 18th century when a Victorian clergyman-writer claimed that she was seen both in the house and among the great beeches around it. The first modern sighting on record occurred in 1938 when the house stood empty and locked. The late William Thomas, former manager of Glendronough Distillery on the borders of the Bognie estate, was in his early teens at the time. One autumn afternoon he was out shooting crows behind the house. Looking up, he saw a pale face surrounded by dark hair, watching him from a window overlooking the courtyard. He called a keeper who also saw the 'intruder'. Armed with their shotguns, the two broke in through a kitchen door and searched the house from top to bottom. There was nobody there, and no sign of forcible entry but their own.

Nearly 10 years later, Mrs Yvonne Morison encountered the ghost.

> It was 28 October. I remember the date because my husband had gone away with the Canadian Army reserve the day before. I was completely alone in the kitchens in the basement – the oldest part. Suddenly in the silence I heard footsteps coming down the staircase from the top of the house. I was

Opposite: the main staircase at Frendraught House. The ghost of Lady Frendraught in a white-and-gold dress has been seen here and on the back stairs, as well as in the grounds of the estate

Opposite below: the silver chalice presented to Forgue Kirk by Sir James three years after the fire. It is said to have been brought to Scotland by Mary Queen of Scots and is the oldest piece of hallmarked silver in the country. Did Sir James give it to the church to ease a guilty conscience?

> terrified, but something made me go to the bottom of the stairs where they eventually entered the kitchen. I peered up into the darkness and remember thinking very strongly – I may even have spoken aloud – 'Well, come on then. If you exist, show yourself.' Perhaps fortunately, the footfalls stopped at the top of the kitchen stairs, and I saw and heard nothing else.

The footsteps were too heavy and clear to be made by mice, she said, and rats had never been seen in the building. 'I knew all the "natural" creaks and groans of the old place. It was none of these.'

Twice the Morisons had guests who cut short their visits because of mysterious disturbances. On both occasions the guests were level-headed people. One was an old army colleague who had been in the thick of the fighting with Mr Morison during the Italian campaign. In both cases their stories matched in every detail, though they had never met. Mrs Morison explained:

> It was quite funny at first. They were a bit embarrassed and it became clear that they thought my husband and I had had a furious fight during the night. When we pointed out that the wall between our bedroom and theirs was 8 feet [2.4 metres] thick and totally soundproof, they became alarmed. They said that they had heard the most dreadful cries for help, with the sound of crashing, like heavy furniture being thrown about, and screams. They had been too terrified to investigate.

Above and left: the present owners of Frendraught House, Yvonne and Alexander Gordon Morison. The Morisons lived at Frendraught for a time after the Second World War, having inherited it in 1942. Mrs Morison had a personal encounter with the ghost of Lady Crichton – as did guests and later tenants

Curse of the chalice

Several guests and subsequent tenants at Frendraught had described seeing a dark lady in a white dress edged and decorated in gold. She was usually standing or walking on the main staircase or the back stairs.

Mr Cryle Shand, genealogist, lawyer, and tenant of Yonder Bognie Farm, has an open mind on the subject of the ghost, but feels that Lady Crichton was more to be pitied than blamed. According to his own theory, she may have been impelled to whatever action she took by a curse – the curse of the chalice that Sir James gave to Forgue Kirk three years after the fire.

> From my research I am almost certain that the cup was one of those brought north by Mary Queen of Scots in the middle of the 16th century: although it is hallmarked 1663 its base is typically pre-Reformation. The Bible says that 'he that eateth and drinketh unworthily, eateth and drinketh damnation unto himself.' Although the Crichtons were nominally a Catholic family, they were a fairly ungodly lot. I believe that Sir James used the sacred chalice for profane purposes – probably for drinking his dram out of – and that the troubles of his family and that of the Gordons who were so closely related to them were brought about by that Biblical damnation. That is why Crichton so piously repented and gave the cup back to the church. That is why it is treated with such respect by the elders of Forgue Kirk to this day. And that is why Dr Arthur Johnson, an 18th-century Scottish Latinist, describes Frendraught as *Tristis et infelix et semper inhospita turris* ('O sad and unhappy and ever inhospitable tower').

There are skulls that create supernatural disturbances because they want to stay in a favourite place. Can such tales be true? This chapter looks at the strange behaviour of the screaming skulls that won't stay buried

Right: the polished skull of Theophilius Broome in its permanent resting place at Chilton Cantelo Manor in Somerset. The skull made 'horrid noises' when anyone tried to bury it

Below: the screaming skull of Bettiscombe Manor in Dorset. As recently as the early 1900s, the skull is said to have taken revenge on someone who tossed it out of the house it loved. Family tradition has it that the relic is the head of a black slave

The skulls that screamed

IN THE QUIET VILLAGE CHURCHYARD of Chilton Cantelo in Somerset, England, picturesque in both name and setting, a lichen-covered tombstone dated 1670 marks the last resting place of one Theophilius Broome – or at least the resting place of most of him. For over 300 years his skull, polished like old ivory, has lain in a cupboard at his former home, Chilton Cantelo Manor. This fulfils a deathbed wish that his head should remain in residence. Not unnaturally, his heirs were uneasy about the idea. But they quickly discovered that attempts to bury the skull with the rest of the body only created problems for everyone.

According to the inscription on Theophilius's tombstone, 'horrid noises, portentive of sad displeasure' were heard throughout the village when attempts were made to rebury his head. These ceased only when the bony relic was disinterred and once more returned to its comfortable cupboard.

Another skull, kept at Wardley Hall near Manchester, is said to be that of a Roman Catholic priest executed for treason in 1641. After being displayed on the tower of a Manchester church, it was recovered by a Catholic family and taken to Wardley. Like its Somerset equivalent, it made noises when removed from the premises. More, it was said to have caused violent thunderstorms. Besides all that, it refused to remain buried. In the chilling words of ghost hunter Eric Maple, it 'always managed to find its own way back [to the house] again'.

Burton Agnes Hall, a beautifully restored Elizabethan mansion in Humberside, contains the skull of Anne Griffith. She was the daughter of Sir Henry Griffith, who built the residence in 1590. Like Theophilius Broome, Anne made the deathbed request that her head be cut off after she died and kept in the house, and the wish was granted. The skull, known locally as 'Owd Nance', was removed on several occasions. Each time it screamed horrifyingly until it was returned to the house. To prevent any further outbreak of such supernatural annoyances, 'Owd Nance' was bricked into the walls of the house itself in 1900 – and Burton Agnes has been mercifully tranquil ever since.

'Screaming skull' legends form a small but curious part of the British folklore tradition. One suggestion is that such stories have their roots in the Romano-British practice of making 'foundation sacrifices' – burying a human or animal victim in the foundations of a house to ensure luck and propitiate the gods. It was perhaps with some knowledge of such practices in mind that Anne Griffith and

Theophilius Broome made their strange requests. Another theory suggests that the stories arose from the rumoured custom of walling up monks and nuns as punishment for breaches of their chastity vows, though in fact such 'executions' were probably rare indeed. A third source could be the Celts. They revered the head in their religion and often preserved severed heads as family treasures or offerings to the gods in sanctuaries. Celtic cult heads of stone have been found in many places in Britain. Whatever their origins, 'screaming skulls' show a uniform objection to being moved from their chosen niches.

One of these 'guardian' skulls has a modern history coming down to the present day. It resides in Bettiscombe Manor near Sherborne in Dorset. Bettiscombe, a fine building of mellow brick and white stone, dates principally from the early 17th century. Parts of it are much older, however, and the land on which it stands has been inhabited since prehistory. The house was built by the Pinney family, who still farm the rich countryside around. Michael Pinney, a noted archaeologist and historian, lives in the manor house itself. His son, Charlie, breeds shire horses for use in film and television work. Both the professional Pinney and his practical son treat their guardian skull with deep respect.

Above: Burton Agnes Hall in Humberside, home of the head of Anne Griffith after her death in the 17th century. The skull was bricked into the walls in 1900 to prevent its ever being touched again – because it screamed terribly when it was moved

Left: Wardley Hall near Manchester. Its resident skull, supposedly that of a Catholic priest, not only screamed but also caused wild thunderstorms when removed from the premises

The earliest written accounts of the skull date from the early 18th century, but the story itself starts in 1685. At that time Azariah Pinney, the squire of Bettiscombe, took part in the Monmouth rebellion. Being on the losing side, he was exiled to the West Indies. As it turned out, his family flourished there, and his grandson, John Frederick Pinney, was able to return to Dorset in style and move back onto the lands of his ancestors. With him came a black slave who became part of the household and was soon a familiar sight in the village. The Negro had been promised that, on his death, his body would be returned by his master to Africa, from where he had been taken by slavers as a child.

But Pinney died first. When the slave died shortly afterwards, no one kept the promise to him and his body was buried in the local churchyard near that of his master. It did not rest content and a mournful wailing seemed to emanate from the grave. Crop failure, cattle disease and storms accompanied the months of moaning. Finally the body was disinterred and the skull taken back to its adopted home in the manor house. There it has remained. In recent years it has nested in a shoe box in Michael Pinney's study, fulfilling the double role of family heirloom and harbinger of doom to any that remove it. According to Pinney:

> It is said to scream and cause agricultural disaster if taken out of the house, and also causes the death, within a year,

of the person who commits the deed. A photographer once carried it as far as the open doorway to take pictures of it, but my wife snatched it back indoors again without anything untoward occurring.

Local lore has it that the last time the skull was 'interfered with', it took its vengeance just as the legend says it would. At the beginning of the 20th century, a tenant who had leased Bettiscombe prior to moving to Australia had a boisterous Christmas party at the manor. During the party he took the skull and hurled it into a horse pond that lay at the side of the house. The following morning the skull was found not in the pond but on the doorstep. How did it get there, when it had to go up a flight of stairs and across a paved patio? One theory, said Michael Pinney, was that

it had been blown there by the wind, but it must have been a very strange and powerful wind. In the Thirties, however, I had an unannounced visit from three young Australians. One of them said that he was the son of the former tenant. His father had indeed died suddenly in Australia within a year of the incident, and his mother had always told him that the skull had brought a curse on them.

Above: skulls placed in the niches of a French Celtic sanctuary as offerings to the gods. Celtic cult heads have been found in many places in Britain and may be a source for the stories of skulls that scream

Kept like an animal

Until alterations were made to the attics of Bettiscombe after the Second World War, the guardian skull had traditionally been kept in a small attic room. The remains of this room can be seen today among the chimney stacks and thick oak rafters under the roof. There is an alternative tale to the black slave legend connected with the attic. This version says that a young girl had been kept prisoner there, bedded on straw like an animal and fed through a grille in the door. Although there is no historical evidence for this story, as there is for John Frederick and his slave, there is a strong family tradition that the skull's 'place' for many years was under the rafters. In the early 1960s, on the track of the Bettiscombe skull, Eric Maple interviewed an old farm worker who claimed to remember 'hearing the skull screaming like a trapped rat in the attic'. Other locals claimed that during thunderstorms there was a rattling sometimes heard in the upper rooms – a rattling made by 'them' playing ninepins with the ancient relic. Exactly who 'they' were was left to the imagination.

Other snippets of lore about the skull seem to have been added on over the years.

A grisly exhibit

Jeremy Bentham, philosopher and political theorist whose reforming zeal helped improve 19th-century life in Britain, shared with the screaming skulls a desire to remain in a favourite place after his death. And he went to elaborate lengths to do so.

Bentham arranged that, when he died, a surgeon friend was to embalm his head and place it upon his skeleton – after the body had been dissected for the teaching of medical students. The skeleton, according to the fun-loving sage's instructions, was dressed in the clothes he had liked best. It was then seated in a glass-fronted upright mahogany box. This was placed in University College,

Michael Pinney and his wife were rather startled when a visitor asked if the skull had 'sweated blood in 1939 before the outbreak of the war, as it had in 1914'.

In fact, the 'screaming skull' of Bettiscombe Manor is probably not that of either the slave or the girl of the legend. In the 1950s, at Pinney's request, it was examined by Professor Gilbert Causey of the Royal College of Surgeons. He pronounced it to be much older than anyone had suspected. It was, he said, the skull of a prehistoric woman, a young girl with delicate features who died between 3000 and 4000 years ago.

So how did it come to be kept at Bettiscombe Manor, and why did such weird legends gather around it?

Death by the sword

There is some evidence of a Romano-British settlement on the site, which points back to the idea of a foundation sacrifice. But if Professor Causey's estimate is correct, the skull pre-dates any house that could have been in the settlement by several hundred years. An interesting parallel can be drawn with the screaming *ghosts* of Reculver in Kent. For many years a legend had persisted that screams and cries heard in woodland around this site of an early Roman settlement were made by the ghosts of children who had been murdered there. In 1964 important archaeological excavations were begun, during the course of which a number of children's skulls and bones were unearthed. One of these bore marks indicating that it had died by the sword. The pathetic skeletons were rather older than the Roman site, some dating from between 1000 and 500 BC.

Pinney himself has come up with a plausible if unusual explanation of the skull's arrival at Bettiscombe Manor: it made its own way there.

Behind the manor, the steep slopes of wooded Pilsdon Pen stretch up far beyond the house's tall chimneys. The tor shows signs of prehistoric fortifications dating from about the same period as Maiden Castle, the great earthworks fortress that lies some miles away to the south-east. Besides containing the remnants of hut circles, the tor is also studded with small burial mounds and cairns. Pinney has excavated some of them through professional interest as an archaeologist. Down from the hilltop trickles a clear stream that travels in an ancient culvert through an outhouse attached to the Bettiscombe kitchens. As Pinney explains:

> I can't prove it, of course, but I rather suspect that the skull was worked loose from the soil at the top of the hill, tumbled into the stream and rolled down the sloping bed of the brook and down into the outhouse here. Such a find would have been traumatic to say the least in a superstitious age. The finder may well have tried to get rid of it, only to feel uneasy about the event – perhaps odd things did occur which convinced him that the skull wished to stay where it had landed. Then the stories began to grow as news of the skull's arrival spread.

The story of the skull at Bettiscombe might easily have reached the ears of old Theophilius Broome at Chilton Cantelo in the adjoining county of Somerset. Perhaps it influenced his decision to arrange that his own head should stay above ground. Whether or not the same idea came to Anne Griffith in what was then Yorkshire from the Bettiscombe tales is anyone's guess.

For their part, Michael Pinney and his family have prospered despite the bizarre relic in the shoe box. So far, however, he has refused to allow the family 'heirloom' to be taken outside the walls of the old manor. 'I'm not superstitious,' he explains with a smile, 'but why risk it?'

Top: Professor Gilbert Causey of the Royal College of Surgeons, who was called in to give an expert opinion on the Bettiscombe skull. He said it was that of a young prehistoric woman – a far cry from the slave of the traditional story

Above: the ruins of Reculver church in Kent, which is connected with local legends about children's ghosts that scream pitifully. Skulls dug up on the site proved to be from an earlier time than the stories indicated – suggesting that 'screaming skull' stories have their origins deep in ancient tradition

London, of which Bentham was a founder and constant supporter. It has remained on a landing of this building near the Gower Street entrance ever since Bentham's death in 1832.

A wax model has replaced the deteriorated head, but the figure still wears the genial philosopher's straw hat and holds his trusty walking stick. A number of witnesses have said that Bentham's ghost, tapping the stone flags with the cane, often walks the corridors near his curious coffin. According to Bill Grundy, the television producer who made a film of Bentham, the ghost 'seems to appear most in times of trouble' – during the 1940 blitz, for example. It is as though the philosopher had appointed himself the 'guardian of University College'.

A short history of hauntings

Above: Nathaniel Hawthorne (1804–1864), the American novelist and short-story writer. His account of the ghost of Dr Harris, which haunted the reading room of Boston's Athenaeum Library (left), is remarkable for its straightforward presentation of the facts

Ghosts seem to take many different forms, appear in the most unlikely places, and haunt all kinds of people. But what exactly are these apparitions? And what causes them? Frank Smyth searches for the answers and surveys some famous phantoms from the past

BEFORE HIS NOVEL *The scarlet letter* made him famous, the American novelist and short-story writer Nathaniel Hawthorne was an official at the Boston Customs House. At this time, in the 1830s, he went every day to the Athenaeum Library to research and write for a few hours. One of the other regulars there was the Reverend Doctor Harris, an octogenarian clergyman who for years had sat in 'his' chair by the fireplace, reading the *Boston Post*.

Hawthorne had never spoken to him, as conversation was strictly forbidden in the reading room, but Dr Harris was almost a fitment of the place, so that Hawthorne felt sure he would have missed him if Dr Harris had not been there. The novelist was, therefore, surprised one evening when a friend told him the old man had died some time previously. He was even more amazed when, the following day, he found the clergyman in his normal chair, reading the newspaper. For weeks Hawthorne continued to see Dr Harris, looking perfectly solid and lifelike.

One of the things that puzzled Hawthorne was the fact that many of the other regulars had been close friends of Dr Harris, though Hawthorne had not. So why did they not see him? Or *did* they see him, but suffer from the same reluctance as Hawthorne to acknowledge his 'presence'? Another factor that puzzled Hawthorne in retrospect was his own unwillingness to touch the figure, or perhaps snatch the newspaper from its hands: 'Perhaps I was loth to destroy the illusion, and to rob myself of so good a ghost story, which might have been explained in some very commonplace way.'

After a while the old gentleman appeared to be watching Hawthorne as if expecting him to 'fall into conversation'.

> But, if so, the ghost had shown the bad judgement common among the spiritual brotherhood, both as regarding the place of interview and the person whom he had selected as recipient of his communications. In the reading room of the Athenaeum, conversation is strictly forbidden, and I couldn't have addressed the apparition without

drawing the instant notice and indignant frowns of the slumberous old gentlemen around me. And what an absurd figure I would have made, solemnly . . . addressing what must have appeared in the eyes of all the rest of the company an empty chair.

'Besides,' concluded Hawthorne in a last appeal to the social proprieties, 'I had never been introduced to Dr Harris.' After some months, Hawthorne entered the Athenaeum to find the haunted chair empty, and he never saw Dr Harris again.

The only drawback to this story as a piece of psychical evidence is that it rests on the testimony of an author who wrote many short stories concerning the supernatural. Hawthorne was a friend of Edgar Allan Poe and Herman Melville, both of whom dealt with the realms of the unknown. On the other hand, he became interested in ghostly phenomena after moving into a house in Massachusetts reputed for years to be haunted. Of this place he wrote: 'I have often, while sitting in the parlour in the daytime, had a perception that somebody was passing the windows – but on looking towards them, nobody is there.'

First class evidence

In neither case – that of his house nor that of Dr Harris – does he appear to have tried to embellish the facts at all, and yet he is acknowledged as a great story writer, accustomed to giving his tales a beginning and a satisfactory end. As a ghost story of fiction, the Dr Harris tale is flat and relatively uninteresting; but as a piece of evidence for an apparition it is first class.

So what was it that Hawthorne saw? To many people the ready answer would be that he saw the earthbound spirit of Dr Harris, somehow trapped in the place that he had been accustomed to 'haunt' in life. Others would say that the ghost was a projection of Hawthorne's memory of the old man, echoing Hamlet's mother's comments on her son's visions: 'This is the very coinage of your brain.' More recently, psychical researchers would suggest that the apparently solid person by the fire was a sort of spiritual 'recording', left by the dead man on his environment, which was somehow received by Hawthorne's mind in much the same way as a television set receives a transmission.

One thing is certain: Nathaniel Hawthorne was far from being alone in seeing a 'ghost' – or what serious parapsychologists and psychical researchers prefer to term an 'apparition'. Since earliest times all civilisations have recorded 'ghosts' – some as a mere generality, a part of folklore, while others have produced specific instances. The difficulty, for the modern observer, is sifting the likely from the less likely instances.

About 500 years earlier, at the beginning of what are loosely known as the 'Dark Ages', a Benedictine monk named Brother John Goby took on a case of psychical research and recorded all the facts with commendable care. Again, although to modern eyes the incident seems bizarre enough at first to be dismissed out of hand, the Goby case was so rare for its time to be worthy of study.

In December 1323, a merchant of Alais, in the south of France, died. His name was Guy de Torno, and within days of his death he was reputed to have returned to haunt his widow in the form of a 'spirit voice'. News of this persistent 'ghost' spread to the town of Avignon, 40 miles (65 kilometres) away, where Pope John XXII then had his residence. (This was during the Great Schism, when two popes, one in Avignon and one in Rome, vied for power.) Pope John was impressed, and appointed Brother John Goby, Prior of the Benedictine Abbey of Alais, to investigate.

Accompanied by three of his fellow Benedictines and about 100 of the town's most respected citizens, Brother John went to the widow's house on Christmas Day and began his investigations. First he examined the house and gardens for any hidden tricks or freak sound effects. Then he posted a guard around the premises to keep out sightseers. The focus of the ghostly manifestations was the bedroom. Goby asked the widow to lie on the bed, along with a 'worthy and elderly woman' while the four monks sat at each corner.

The monks then recited the Office for the Dead, and soon became aware of a sweeping sound in the air, like the brushing of a stiff

Below: Edgar Allan Poe (1809–1849), master writer of the macabre short story. He was a friend of Nathaniel Hawthorne, and it is possible that he could have participated in the 'creation' of the ghost of Dr Harris at the Athenaeum Library

Below: 'Marley's ghost appears to Scrooge' from Dickens's *A Christmas carol*. Doomed to walk the earth to atone for his ill-spent life, 'Marley' warns that Scrooge too will be condemned unless he mends his ways

Above: Pope John XXII, who directed a Benedictine prior, Brother John Goby, to investigate the 'ghost of Alais' in 1323

Below: Prince Rupert leads his cavalry into the first major battle of the English Civil War at Edgehill in 1642. For months afterwards, people claimed to have seen a ghostly re-enactment of the battle; among those reported to have taken part was Prince Rupert himself – but he was still alive

broom. The widow cried out in terror. Goby asked aloud if the noise was made by the dead man, and a thin voice answered: 'Yes, I am he.'

At this point some of the townspeople were admitted to the room as witnesses, and stood in a circle round the bed. The voice assured them that it was not an emissary of the Devil – the usual assumption in medieval times – but the earthbound ghost of Guy de Torno, condemned to haunt its old home because of the sins it had committed there. It said that it had every hope of getting to heaven once its period of purgatory was over. It also told Brother John that it knew he was carrying the Sacrament in a pyx – a silver box in which the Host is carried – concealed under his robes. This was a fact known only to Goby. The spirit added that its prime sin had been adultery, which carried the penalty of excommunication from the Sacrament in those days. The spirit then 'sighed and departed'.

Brother John wrote out his report and despatched it to the Pope at Avignon. The incident's abiding interest to psychical research lies in the objectivity with which the investigation was carried out. Of course it was not perfect and does leave a number of questions unanswered. The 'sweeping' noise and the 'sigh' might well have been a result of the Mistral, the mournful wind that blows across that part of France in the winter. The 'voice' itself may have been produced by ventriloquism on the part of the widow – consciously or unconsciously – particularly if she suspected her husband of infidelity and wanted to discredit his memory. Against this, however, has to be weighed the fact that, had she been discovered in such trickery, she stood a very real chance of being accused of witchcraft and suffering death at the stake.

Another impressive investigation, this time of a 'mass apparition', was conducted in 1644 by a number of level-headed army officers and remains an enigma: either they were all lying, or something untoward did indeed happen. On 23 October 1642, Royalist troops under Prince Rupert of the Rhine, nephew of King Charles I, and Parliamentarians under Robert Devereux, third Earl of Essex fought the first serious battle of the English Civil War at Edgehill, Warwickshire. After the indecisive clash the bodies of some 2000 men lay on the unseasonably frozen slopes of Edgehill.

A month after the battle, a number of local shepherds saw what they at first thought was another fight at the same spot: the thundering cavalry, rolling gunsmoke, flashing steel. And they also heard the neighing of horses, the screams of the wounded and the steady beat of drums. It was only when the whole tableau suddenly vanished that they took fright and ran to tell the authorities in the nearby town. On Christmas Eve the phantom battle was enacted again, and was so convincing that a London printer, Thomas Jackson, interviewed several witnesses and published an acount of the phenomenon in pamphlet form on 4 January 1643.

This was drawn to the attention of the King, who was so intrigued that despite his hard-pressed military position he appointed half a dozen army officers to investigate on his behalf. They were led by Colonel Sir Lewis Kirk, former governor of the garrison at Oxford, and a young cavalry captain named Dudley who had ridden at Edgehill.

On their return the officers brought detailed confirmation of the news. Not only had they interviewed the shepherds and recorded their accounts, but on two occasions they had seen the battle themselves, recognising not only a number of the men who had died on the field, but also Prince Rupert, who was still very much alive. Whether or not anyone took notice of it at the time, this last fact carried with it the intriguing suggestion that the phenomenon was a sort of action replay rather than haunting by revenant spirits.

Although Sir Lewis and his colleagues were justifiably startled, they drew no conclusions, merely reporting the facts of what they had seen. There was no obvious reason for them to lie: their evidence might have pleased the King or upset him. As it chanced he took the incident as a good omen – wrongly, as it turned out, for six years later he was beheaded.

The ghostly man in grey

A recent example of an apparition witnessed on innumerable occasions by literally dozens of people is that provided by the so-called 'man in grey' who is recorded as appearing at the Theatre Royal in Drury Lane, London, from the early 18th century until the late 1970s. The accounts are remarkably consistent, although the 'stagey' look of the ghost and the fact that it appears in a theatre has convinced more than one witness that they were seeing an actor dressed for a part.

The figure is that of a man of above average height with a strong, handsome face. He wears a three-cornered hat, powdered wig, long grey cloak, sword and riding boots, and emerges from a wall on the left hand side of the upper circle, walks around behind the seats, and vanishes into the opposite wall. He has never been known to speak or pay any attention to witnesses, and although he seems perfectly solid, if his way is barred by a living person he dissolves and then reappears on the other side of them.

The identity of the 'man in grey' has never been satisfactorily proven, but a possible clue turned up in the late 1840s, when workmen were making alterations to the wall from which he appears. In a bricked-up alcove they found the seated skeleton of a man, with a rusty dagger between his ribs. A few tattered remnants of cloth clung to the figure but crumbled to dust when touched. At the obligatory inquest it was suggested that the man may have been a victim of Christopher Ricks, the 'bad man of old Drury' who had managed the theatre in the time of Queen Anne and was notorious for his violence. Ricks made constant alterations to the theatre's structure, and could easily have disposed of a body without too much difficulty. However, there was no solid evidence, and after an open verdict was returned the body was given a pauper's funeral at a nearby graveyard.

Top: this is not, as it may seem, final evidence for the existence of ghosts, but a carefully staged visitation photographed for the British Tourist Authority at London's Theatre Royal, Drury Lane. The ghostly apparition is the so-called 'man in grey', a spectre said to have haunted the theatre for over 200 years. Even in reality it obligingly appeared for the critic and historian W. J. McQueen Pope (above) when he was conducting sightseers round the theatre

However, the 'man in grey' continued to be seen throughout the Victorian era and on into the 20th century. W. J. McQueen Pope, theatre critic and historian, saw the ghost many times and made ardent but fruitless attempts to establish its identity. An interesting point was that the ghost appeared regularly in the period between the mid 1930s and Pope's death in 1960, while he was conducting sightseers around the Theatre Royal. On every occasion, the visitors saw the ghost too, many of them signing testimonials to this effect.

This fact raises a salient question in the minds of psychical researchers: did Pope serve as an unconscious catalyst for the apparition? We know that people differ in their ability both to perceive psychic phenomena and to project apparitions to others. If Pope was gifted in both respects, was the vision of his visitors somehow stimulated by him? Did he, in some way, summon up the 'man in grey'?

Certainly he did not invent the ghost, and its last recorded sighting, by an American who thought he was seeing an actor during an afternoon matinée, took place in 1977, 17 years after Pope's death. But it is certain that the spectre appeared most frequently during Pope's association with the Theatre Royal.

The Pope puzzle presents just one more baffling aspect of the complex phenomenon known to parapsychology as 'apparitions'..

Ghosts without souls?

If ghosts are spirits of the dead, as many believe, how can we account for the 'soulless' apparitions – such as those of animals, buses and other inanimate objects – that have been seen?

IN THE MIDDLE of the 1930s a large red London bus bearing a number 7 route number harassed motorists in the North Kensington area of London. The junction of St Mark's Road and Cambridge Gardens in that area had long been considered a dangerous corner – it was 'blind' from both roads – and had caused numerous accidents.

The decision of the local authority to straighten out the bend was partially influenced by the testimony of late night motorists, who claimed that they had crashed at the junction while swerving to avoid a speeding double decker bus that hurtled down St Mark's Road in the small hours, long after regular buses ceased service.

A typical report to the Kensington police read: 'I was turning the corner and saw a bus tearing towards me. The lights of the top and bottom decks and the headlights were full on but I could see no sign of crew or passengers. I yanked my steering wheel hard over, and mounted the pavement, scraping the roadside wall. The bus just vanished.'

After one fatal accident, during which a driver had swerved and hit the wall head on, an eyewitness told the coroner's inquest that he had seen the mystery bus hurtling towards the car seconds before the driver spun off the road. When the coroner expressed what was perhaps natural cynicism, dozens of local residents wrote to his office and to the local newspapers offering to testify that they had seen the 'ghost bus'. Among the most impressive of these witnesses was a local transport official who claimed that he had seen the vehicle draw up to the bus depot in the early hours of the morning, stand with engine purring for a moment, and then disappear.

The mystery was never solved, but it is perhaps significant that the 'ghost' bus was not seen after the danger of the sharp corner was removed, and it was suggested that the vision was 'projected' onto the spot to dramatise the inherent danger of the intersection. If so, by whom? And if, as was also suggested, it was in the minds of the motorists themselves – a sort of natural projection of their fears at the corner – how did they manage to superimpose it on the vision of the passers-by, not to mention that of the bus depot official who saw it from an entirely different angle?

In fact, the phantom motor bus of Kensington epitomises a problem that for centuries has faced those who believe that ghosts

Right: the tale of this phantom ship was reported by the American minister and author Dr Cotton Mather in his book *Wonders of the invisible world* (1702). The ship set sail from America but never reached its destination in England, and nothing was ever heard of it again. Some months later, however, spectators at the port from which it sailed saw what seemed to be the self-same ship appear in a cloud; then it keeled over and simply disappeared

Below: the junction of St Mark's Road and Cambridge Gardens in Kensington, London, became renowned in the 1930s for the mysterious double decker bus that travelled at great speed in that area in the middle of the night – when no buses were in service

are revenant spirits. If a ghost is the 'soul' of a dead person returned to earth, how do we account for phantom buses – and of course their lineal ancestors phantom coaches, which feature so heavily in folklore?

Come to that, why do returning spirits not appear in the nude – for with very few reliably recorded exceptions, none do? As Lyall Watson succinctly puts it in his book *Supernature*: 'While I am prepared in principle to concede the possibility of an astral body, I cannot bring myself to believe in astral shoes and shirts and hats.'

'Ghostly' lore is strewn with stories of inanimate objects suddenly becoming apparent to the sense of observers, from the 'phantom' accordion accredited to Daniel Dunglas Home, the 19th-century Spiritualist, to Macbeth's dagger. In the latter case William Shakespeare, writing in an age steeped in superstition, seems to have been as aware of the anomaly of 'spirit objects' as he was of almost every other field of human experience: '. . . art thou, O fateful dagger, sensible to feeling as to sight, or art thou but a dagger of the mind, a false creation, proceeding from the heat oppressed brain?'

One of the most convincing stories of totally 'soulless' apparitions is recorded in the day book of the Tower of London – a place that according to popular belief is saturated with ghosts. The man who made the entry was Edmund Lenthal Swifte, who in 1814 was appointed Keeper of the Crown Jewels and continued in the office until 1842, a total of 28 years. The account of what he saw on a Sunday evening in October 1817 is best left to him.

> I was at supper with my wife, our little boy, and my wife's sister in the sitting room of the Jewel House, which is said to have been the 'doleful prison' of Anne Boleyn and of the ten bishops whom Oliver Cromwell piously accommodated there. The doors were all closed, heavy and dark curtains were let down over the windows, and the only light in the room was that of two candles on the table. I sat at the foot of the table, my son on my right, my wife fronting the chimney piece, and her sister on the opposite side. I had offered a glass of wine and water to my wife, when on putting it to her lips she paused, and exclaimed, 'Good God! what is that?'
>
> I looked up, and saw a cylindrical figure, like a glass tube, something about the thickness of my arm, and hovering between the ceiling and table; its contents appeared to be a dense fluid, white and pale azure . . . incessantly rolling and mingling within the cylinder. This lasted about two minutes, when it began to move before my sister-in-law, following the oblong shape of the table, before my son and myself. Passing behind my wife it paused for a moment over her right shoulder (observe there was no mirror opposite in which she could then behold it.) Instantly she crouched down, and with both hands covering her shoulder, shrieked out, 'Oh Christ! It has seized me!'
>
> Even now as I write I feel the horror of that moment. I caught up my chair striking at the 'appearance' with a blow that hit the wainscot behind her. It then crossed the upper end of the table and disappeared in the recess of the opposite window.

There was no recurrence of this curious manifestation, but some years later it did help Swifte's judgement of a soldier in the Tower who actually died from fright of what he had seen outside Swifte's 'front door'.

The soldier had been on sentry-go outside the Jewel House when, at around midnight, he had heard a guttural snarl behind him and turned to see a huge black bear, reared up on

In his book *Supernature* Lyall Watson (below) suggests that the fact that ghosts appear as people remember them indicates that apparitions are part of a mental process rather than a supernatural one. Certainly most ghosts do appear fully clothed or are dressed in a shroudlike garment, as was the ghost that terrorised the residents of Hammersmith, London, in the early 1800s (bottom)

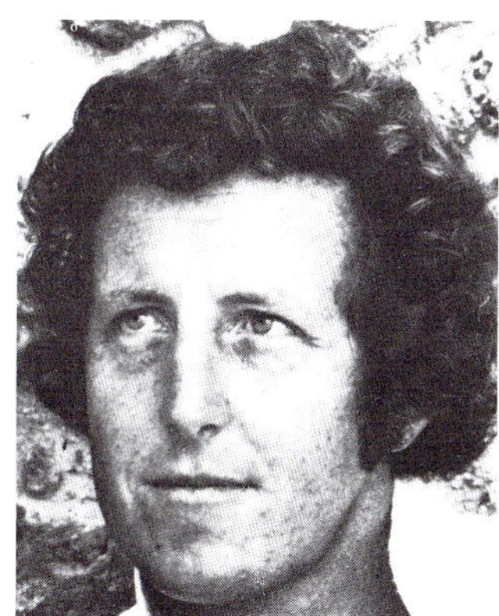

its hind legs, fangs bared, eyes red with rage, and talons groping towards him. The soldier rammed his bayonet into the belly of the animal, but the weapon passed clean through and the apparition disappeared.

A patrol found the soldier a few moments later, senseless. The bayonet, with a heavy 'Tower issue' musket attached, was embedded in the solid wood of the door. The soldier was taken, still insensible, to the guardroom, where a doctor pronounced that he was neither drunk nor asleep, and the following morning Swifte interviewed him; over and over the soldier repeated his bizarre tale until, three days later, he died.

For about 300 years, until the middle of the 17th century, the Tower housed a royal menagerie, and among the animals recorded as having been kept were a number of bears. Although no account of an autopsy on the soldier survives, the fact that he died three days after his experience could indicate that he was ill without knowing it, and that the apparition was an hallucination caused by his illness. On the other hand, animal ghosts make more sense as 'revenant spirits' than their human counterparts, for the reason already given; they at least 'appear' exactly as in life. The fact that Man has lost most of his 'primitive' instincts while animals retain theirs may also have an as-yet unexplained bearing on their 'paranormal' role.

Above: the Jewel House in the Tower of London where Edmund Swifte and his family were troubled by a cylindrical form filled with blue and white fluid

Below: phantom horses, complete with riders, are a common form of haunting, and are usually associated with a particular place. Possibly they are a kind of recording of a highly emotional or dramatic event, which is 'replayed' in certain circumstances

A phantom pig

Stories of phantom dogs are common to the United States, Europe, and many parts of Africa. Ghostly horses, cattle, and even sheep have their part in folklore, and although, like all folk tales, the accounts of their appearances have undoubtedly become distorted in the telling over centuries, some are eerily convincing. In 1908 the British Society for Psychical Research (SPR) made exhaustive enquiries into the appearance of what appeared to be a phantom pig in the

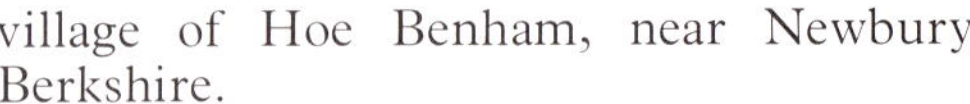

village of Hoe Benham, near Newbury, Berkshire.

On 2 November 1907, two young men named Oswald Pittman and Reginald Waud were painting in the garden of their house, Laburnum Villa. At 10 a.m. Pittman got up to speak to the milkman and saw his friend Miss Clarissa Miles coming up the lane; she was due to join the men for a painting session. Accompanying her like a pet dog was a large white pig with an unusually long snout. When Pittman told Waud about it, Waud asked him to tell Miss Miles to keep the animal outside and close the garden gate securely – Waud was a keen gardener and did not want it among his plants. However, when Miss Miles arrived she was alone, and denied all knowledge of the animal. If it had been following her, she pointed out, she would surely have heard it grunting and pattering. However, she and Pittman went back up the lane and asked several children if they had seen a pig that day; none of them had done so. The following morning the milkman, pressed by a bewildered Pittman, signed a statement to the effect that he had not seen a pig, and he pointed out that in any case the area was under a swine fever curfew, and any stray animal would be destroyed.

Pittman and Waud went to London for a few months and while there reported the odd incident to a member of the SPR. When they returned to Hoe Benham in February, however, the story of Pittman's apparition had become widespread, and shedding their natural reserve the villagers inundated them with stories of previous 'phantoms'. Local theory had it that they all stemmed from the suicide of a farmer named Tommy King whose farm, which was demolished in 1892, had bordered the lane. Investigation of the parish records showed there had been two Tommy Kings, one dying in 1741 and the other in 1753, but there was no indication of which one was the suicide. An old man named John Barrett testified that when he was a boy in 1850 he had been returning with seven or eight men in a hay cart along the lane when 'a white thing' appeared in the air. All the men had seen it, and the horses obviously had too, for they went wild.

'This thing kept a-bobbin' and a-bobbin' and the horses kept a-snortin' and a-snortin'' until the wagon reached the neighbourhood of King's Farm, when the shape vanished. In 1873, at the same spot, Barrett had seen a creature 'like a sheep' pawing the ground in the lane. He took a blow at it with his stick, but it disappeared before the stick landed.

Another man, Albert Thorne, said that in the autumn of 1904 he heard 'a noise like a whizzin' of leaves, and saw summat like a calf knuckled down' about $2\frac{1}{2}$ feet (75 centimetres) high and 5 feet (1.5 metres) long, with glowing eyes. As he watched, it faded away. Yet another witness, unnamed, said that, in bright moonlight in January 1905, he had

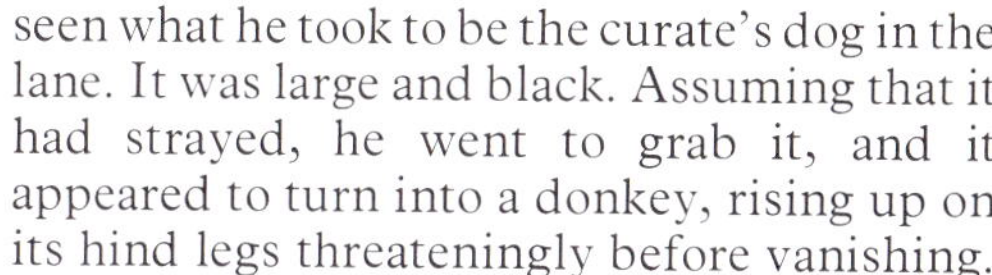

seen what he took to be the curate's dog in the lane. It was large and black. Assuming that it had strayed, he went to grab it, and it appeared to turn into a donkey, rising up on its hind legs threateningly before vanishing.

Pittman, Waud, and Miss Miles reported one more experience. While walking in the lane, Miss Miles was suddenly overcome by an irrational fear, and told her companions that she felt the presence of an evil being, charged with malice towards them. She also felt that she was suffocating. As they reached the spot where Pittman had seen the pig, all three heard an 'unearthly scream', although no one else was about. Waud, who had been sceptical from the beginning, was finally convinced that the ghostly animal existed by this cry from nowhere.

Okehampton Castle in Devon, England. A 17th-century phantom coach, constructed of the bones of the four husbands of the 'Wicked Lady Howard' – all of whom she is said to have murdered – travels the road that runs across the moor from Tavistock to Okehampton. The ashen, sheeted spectre of Lady Howard rides inside the coach and a skeleton hound runs before it. According to legend, each night the hound must pick a blade of grass from Okehampton Park to take back to Lady Howard's family home at Tavistock – a penance that must be endured until every blade of grass is picked

Animal investigators

The sensitivity of animals, particularly cats and dogs, to paranormal phenomena is almost a truism. Dr Robert Morris of Kentucky, a parapsychologist who used animals as 'controls' in his experiments in the 1960s, reported his investigation of a haunted house in one room of which a tragedy had occurred. He used a dog, cat, rat, and rattlesnake.

> The dog upon being taken about two or three feet [less than a metre] into the room immediately snarled at its owner and backed out of the door. No amount of cajoling could prevent the dog from struggling to get out and it refused to re-enter. The cat was brought into the room carried in its owner's arms. When the cat got a similar distance into the room, it immediately leaped upon the owner's shoulders, dug in, then leaped to the ground, orienting itself towards a chair. It spent several minutes hissing and spitting and staring at the unoccupied chair in a corner of the room until it was finally removed . . .
>
> [The rattlesnake] immediately assumed an attack posture focusing on the same chair that had been of interest to the cat. After a couple of minutes it slowly moved its head toward a window, then moved back and then receded into its alert posture about five minutes later . . .

The rat was the only creature not to react at all, but all four animals were tested in a separate room some time later, and there behaved normally.

In the misty world of apparitions, no one, not even the most dedicated psychical researcher, knows quite what is the motivation behind them. What we do know is that they are not confined to human beings; the 'ghosts' of both animals and inanimate objects have been lucidly recorded over the years, even including the 'soul' of a London Transport bus.

Understanding ghosts

The troubled spirits of the dead, phantom animals, spectral coaches – all these have been called 'ghosts'. But are they all the same? We can learn a great deal from what hauntings have in common – and how they differ

THE PERENNIAL QUESTION as to whether ghosts exist must, in view of various surveys carried out by such bodies as the British Society for Psychical Research (SPR) over the last 100 years or so, be answered in the affirmative. To reject the testimony of the many hundreds of respectable people who claim to have experienced apparitions as wishful thinking, self-delusion or downright lying would be sheer wilfulness.

The question facing modern parapsychologists and psychophysical researchers is: *how* do ghosts exist? Are they revenant spirits? Are they the result of telepathy? Are they produced by mass hallucination or self-hypnosis? Advances in psychology over the last few decades have brought us nearer to understanding some aspects of apparitions, but the definitive truth still eludes us.

The most common form of 'ghost' appears to be the 'crisis apparition', which occurs when a person under great stress – sometimes on the point of death – appears to someone close to them as a 'vision' or, occasionally, as a disembodied voice.

The majority of crisis apparition cases have tragic overtones. For instance, soldiers have appeared to their mothers or wives at the exact time of their own deaths on faraway battlefields. But not all do so.

Victoria Branden, in her book *Understanding ghosts*, quotes the case of a friend who was evacuated from England to Canada during the Second World War because of a health problem, leaving her husband behind in the Services. One evening, the children were busy with their homework, while their mother was ironing in what she admitted to Mrs Branden was 'a rather dreamlike state'.

Suddenly she saw the door of the room open, and her uniformed husband came in. Before she could recover from her astonishment, he vanished. She put down the iron and sat, near to fainting, in a chair. The children clustered around her anxiously and when she told them what had happened they said that they had not seen anything and the door certainly had not opened. The mother and the elder child had, however, read of crisis apparitions and became convinced that the vision meant that the husband had been killed or injured. They made a note of the time and circumstances, but agonisingly, that was all they could do.

Some days later, to what must have been their enormous relief, news came: the husband had been unexpectedly chosen to go on a training programme to Canada, at a camp very near to his family. This meant, of course, that he could live with them while abroad. When the couple were finally reunited the husband said that the news had come as a happy shock. He could not remember consciously 'projecting' any thought to his wife, but they worked out that he had probably opened his commanding officer's door after hearing the news at about the same time as the wife had 'seen' her door open.

An interesting point about this incident is that the wife was 'rather dreamlike' at the time, with her mind in an open and receptive state. The children, who saw nothing, were concentrating hard on their homework.

Exactly how telepathic information is communicated remains a mystery, particularly so in the case where an apparition

This photograph of the library at Combermere Abbey in Cheshire was taken on 5 December 1891 by Sybell Corbet, who had been staying at the house. When she developed the plate, she was startled to see the shape of an elderly gentleman sitting in a chair on the left of the picture. The figure was later identified as that of Lord Combermere himself: but at the time the photograph was taken, he was being buried a few miles away

appears solid and living. However, scientists point out that perception is a much more complex business than at first appears: vivid dreams, for instance, often appear perfectly solid and physical, and in such cases the percipient is not receiving information through his eyes. A hypnotist may tell a subject that when he or she awakes only the hypnotist will be in the room – even though other people may be present. When the subject comes around he will not see the others present until the hypnotist removes the suggestion. Something like this may happen in cases of telepathy, although it seems remarkable that the agent – or person 'sending' the hallucination – can achieve at a distance, and in many cases while he is unconscious, what the hypnotist can only manage by giving specific instructions.

Evidence points to the fact that the agent's mind plays a smaller part in crisis apparitions than does that of the percipient. If we look at recorded cases it becomes apparent that the agent rarely appears as he is at the moment of 'transmission' – the percipient does not see a mangled body in a motor car, or a dying wounded soldier in a trench, but what appears to be a normal image of the agent that, moreover, relates to the percipient's surroundings.

This point is stressed by G. N. M. Tyrrell in his book *Apparitions*. He points out that apparitions in crisis cases have been guilty of such unghostlike phenomena as casting shadows or appearing reflected in a mirror.

> [They] adapt themselves almost miraculously to the physical conditions of the percipient's surroundings, of which the agent as a rule can know little or nothing. These facts reveal the apparition to be a piece of stage machinery which the percipient must have a large hand in creating and some of the details for which he must supply – that is to say, an apparition cannot be merely a direct expression of the agent's *idea*; it must be a drama worked out with that idea as its *motif*.

But telepathy can only partly explain cases of collective apparitions, where a group of people witness the same thing. And it is hard to see how it could play any part in the case of, for instance, the phantom London Transport bus (see page 68) for by definition the telepathic agent must be a sentient being. One of the most famous cases of a collective apparition was reported to the SPR in the late 19th century by Charles Lett, the son-in-law of a Captain Towns of Sydney. One day at about 9 p.m. some six weeks after the Captain's death, his daughter, Mrs Lett, and a Miss Berthon entered a bedroom at his home. The gas light was burning:

> And they were amazed to see, reflected in the polished surface of the wardrobe, the image of Captain Towns. It was . . . like an ordinary medallion portrait, but life-size. The face appeared wan and pale . . . and he wore a kind of grey flannel jacket, in which he had been accustomed to sleep. Surprised and half alarmed at what they saw, their first idea was that a portrait had been hung in the room and that what they saw was its reflection – but there was no picture of the kind. Whilst they were looking and wondering, my wife's sister, Miss Towns, came into the room and before any of the others had time to speak she exclaimed: 'Good gracious! Do you see Papa!'
>
> One of the housemaids passing by was called into the room. Immediately she cried: 'Oh miss! The Master!' The captain's own servant, the butler, and the nurse were also called in and immediately recognised him. Finally Mrs Towns was sent for and, seeing the

Below: cases of crisis apparitions are most common in times of war, when a mother may see her son at the moment of his death on a battlefield. It seems that the shock of death causes some kind of telepathic communication between son and mother. But rarely does the mother have a vision of a dying soldier; in most cases she sees her son as he appeared in normal, everyday life

Left: when Mr Bootman, a bank manager pursuing his hobby of photographing church architecture, took this picture at Eastry, Kent, in 1956, his wife and a cleaning woman were the only other people present. But the ghostly form of a vicar somehow appeared on the film. Some years later Mr Bootman showed the photograph to a Women's Institute group and was told that a similar phantom had been seen in the same church in the 1940s. This may well be an example of what is called a 'place-centred' ghost: the vicar's strong attachment to the church could have led to a 'record' of his image being imprinted upon it

> apparition, she advanced towards it with her arm extended as if to touch it, and as she passed her hand over the panel of the wardrobe the figure gradually faded away, and never again appeared.

Those parapsychologists who lean to the telepathic origin of all apparitions would probably say that the vision was seen first by either Mrs Letts or Miss Berthon, who then passed it on by thought transference to each arrival. But the question remains: where did the vision come from in the first place?

One of the early SPR pioneers, F. W. H. Myers, author of the book *Human personality and its survival of bodily death*, suggested that it was the revenant spirit or 'essence' of Captain Towns taking a last look at his old home six weeks after death. Myers said that an apparition 'may be a manifestation of persistent personal energy' and quoted several cases to illustrate his point.

In one a travelling salesman, Mr F.G., arrived at a hotel in Boston, Massachusetts,

The ghost that grew and grew

One of the main problems facing the objective psychical researcher is that of sheer human gullibility. People like a good ghost story and tend to embellish the narrative, so that after a few retellings the stark facts of the case become wrapped up in a cocoon of invention.

In the summer of 1970 the author of this series, Frank Smyth, who was at that time an associate editor of the magazine *Man, Myth and Magic*, tried an experiment to examine the form taken by this gullibility. He *invented* a ghost, complete with location, background and 'witnesses' and published the story in the magazine.

The invention was completely random. One Sunday morning Smyth had gone down to London's dockland to meet John Philby, son of super-spy 'Kim' Philby. Philby's building company was renovating a site at Ratcliffe Wharf, and Smyth decided that the deserted dock was sufficiently eerie to provide a location for his ghost. Hard by Ratcliffe Wharf is the semi-derelict church of St Anne, and this, plus the fact that it was a Sunday morning, decided Smyth to make his 'ghost' that of a clergyman. Alongside the wharf runs Ratcliffe Highway, once – at least until the late 19th century – a thoroughfare of brothels, grog shops, and cheap boarding houses. The proximity of this old road suggested to Smyth that his vicar had been the owner of a sailor's rooming house, and that he had robbed 'homeward-bounders' (seamen newly paid off from ships in the Thames), had killed them in their lodgings, and disposed of their bodies in the river. Thus the background was set up.

Philby, himself a former war correspondent, and Smyth then decided that witnesses were important. They and one of Philby's employees lent their names to the fiction that they had seen the ghost – the figure of an old white haired man with a walking stick. They also agreed that if anyone, either researcher or interested enquirer, asked about the 'phenomenon' they would immediately confess that it was invented.

Smyth then wrote the story as a 'factual' article in *Man, Myth and Magic*. No one ever queried the credentials of the 'Phantom Vicar of Ratcliffe Wharf' but over the next twelve months or so eight books purporting to tell the stories of genuine ghosts appeared, each featuring the phantom vicar. Only one, by a London *Sunday Times* feature writer, treated the subject with some scepticism; the others not only recounted the tale without comment but one, by a well-known writer on the supernatural, actually embellished it.

In 1973 Smyth wrote an article telling of his experiment for the *Sunday Times*, and subsequently appeared in a BBC-2 film produced from Bristol entitled *A leap in the dark*. This film, too, told the story of the invention, but it also featured a number of people who claimed actually to have *seen* the phantom vicar. One man said that he had witnessed an old man in 18th-century clerical garb walking in the roadway outside the 'Town of Ramsgate' pub, near St Katherine's Dock – a good half mile from Ratcliffe Wharf. The writer Jilly Cooper told of interviewing a police superintendent who, on retirement from the River Branch of the Metropolitan force, had said that as a young man he had been unwilling to enter Ratcliffe Wharf for fear of the ghostly priest. A Thames waterman claimed that he had seen the shadowy form of the vicar standing on Ratcliffe Wharf some months before the story appeared in the magazine. After the television programme many other letters were sent to the BBC's Bristol office, most of them apparently sincere, telling of sightings.

There is absolutely no foundation for the Ratcliffe Wharf story. Nowhere in the record of Wapping – or indeed any other part of London's dockland – does there feature any tale of a ghostly cleric. One psychical researcher suggested that Smyth's ghost may have existed, and somehow made itself felt to him. The fact is that apparently reasonable people still claim to see the apparition in the area – despite its widespread refutation.

one afternoon and sat working in his room. He suddenly became aware of a presence and looked up to see his sister, who had died nine years previously. As he sprang delightedly to his feet and called her name she vanished, and yet he had time to take in every detail. 'She appeared as if alive,' he said, but added that there was a small red scratch on her right cheek.

Disturbed, Mr F.G. made an unscheduled stop at his parents' home and told them of his experience. When he mentioned the scratch, his mother was overcome with emotion, and said that she had made the scratch on the dead body of her daughter accidentally, as she was preparing it for burial. Two weeks later, the mother died.

Myers wrote that the figure was 'not the corpse with the dull mark on which the mother's regretful thoughts might dwell, but . . . the girl in health and happiness, with the symbolic *red* mark worn simply as a test of identity.' He suggested that the apparition was the spirit of the dead girl inducing her brother to go home and see their mother before she died.

Where an apparition persistently 'haunts' a place or a house – or sometimes even a person – believers in an afterlife assert that the spirit is trapped in its earthly environment, perhaps because of some unfulfilled task, or for the purpose of punishment. Unfortunately, unlike the ghosts of well-rounded fiction, these 'haunting' apparitions do not seem to make much sense in their actions; like Nathaniel Hawthorne's Dr Harris (see page 64), they carry on in a mundane fashion, either wandering about or simply staring out of windows.

By and large parapsychologists as a whole, however, tend to theorise that in certain cases a kind of psychic record may be imprinted on a location, perhaps because of some violence or strong emotion generated there. In these cases, the apparition would not be a sentient spirit, a 'mind', but merely a projection like a cinema film. This certainly seems to be the most likely explanation of, for instance, the Edgehill haunting (see page 64). It also ties in with the telepathy theories; if a person can send an image of himself telepathically to a percipient, may he not also be able to send a sort of 'free floating' image that hangs, as it were, in the atmosphere to be picked up by anyone sensitive enough to receive it?

Such a concept would also explain the occasionally convincing 'photographs' of apparitions; in such cases the photographic film may be more sensitive to the surroundings than its operator; conversely, where a photographer sees a ghost and his camera fails to do so, he may be hypersensitive.

If such phantom recordings are possible, it may be that they are not necessarily fixed for ever. Andrew Green, in his book *Ghost hunting*, quotes an interesting case of a woman in red shoes, red dress and a black head-dress reported to haunt a mansion in 18th-century England. In the early 19th century it was reported that the apparition was that of a lady in pink shoes, pink dress, and a grey head-dress. She was not witnessed again until the mid 19th century, when the figure had dwindled down to 'a lady in a white gown and with grey hair'. Just before the Second World War, all that was reported was 'the sound of a woman walking along the corridor and the swish of her dress'. In 1971, shortly before the demolition of the property involved, workmen felt 'a presence in one of the old corridors'.

All these explanations may account for the mysterious sightings of apparently solid, living beings where no such beings should be. Or perhaps none of them do. Modern scientific research – into, for instance, the baffling field of quantum physics – constantly produces new slants on old phenomena. Ghosts – whether human or non-human – may yet prove to belong to a sphere of reality so far undreamed of in our philosophy.

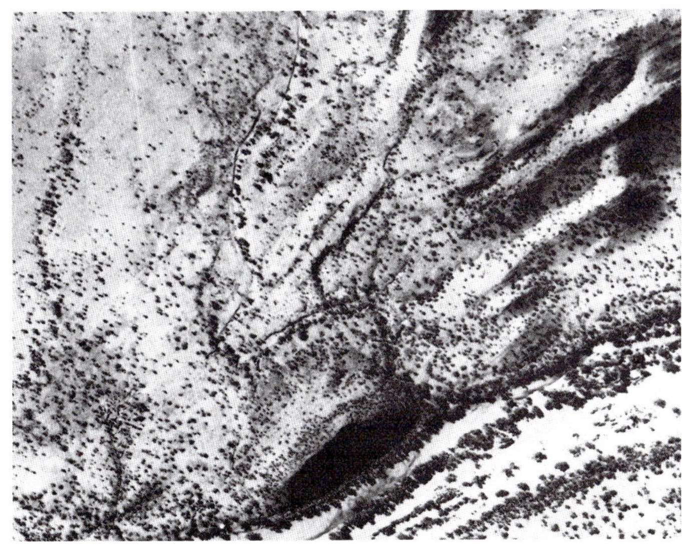

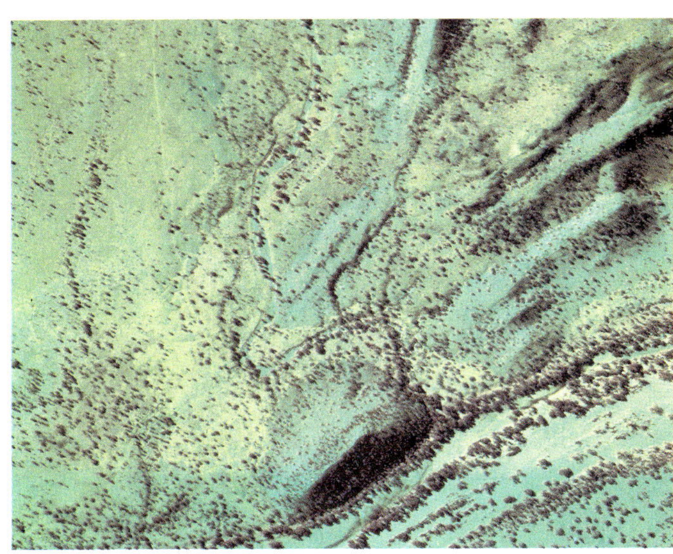

Ghost photographs often show images unseen by the human eye, as film is inherently more sensitive to certain light frequencies. The difference is rather like that between a picture shot with a standard film (left) and one taken with infra-red equipment (right). The infra-red photograph shows this tract of Australian desert more clearly and with much sharper detail, and provides information not otherwise available

In search of apparitions

No two ghosts are alike – and a good ghost hunter will approach each haunting differently. Serious researchers have developed special techniques for gathering and documenting the kind of evidence they seek

'FEAR CAME UPON ME, and trembling, which made all my bones to shake. Then a spirit passed before my face; the hair of my flesh stood up. It stood still, but I could not discern the form thereof.'

This is how the experience of seeing a ghost is described in the Book of Job 4: 14–16. The word 'ghost' comes from an ancient root meaning 'to be scared', and to many, including Job, encounters with ghosts have been literally hair-raising. Fortunately, some people, far from being frightened, are willing to seek out ghosts and actively investigate them.

The existence of ghosts has been accepted without question in almost all cultures throughout history. Only with the growth of the scientific outlook in the West in the last few centuries have their existence and nature been disputed. But serious attempts to find out what they are and to study their behaviour are surprisingly few. And many people still respond to the idea of ghosts with an irrational blend of fear, ridicule and laughter. We reject what we do not understand, rather than face the possibility that there are indeed more things in heaven and earth than are dreamed of, let alone taken seriously, by the scientific establishment.

Ghosts are even rejected by people who have seen them. 'I saw it, but I still don't believe it!' is a commonly reported reaction, for the human mind instinctively rejects information it cannot assimilate and interpret. Clearly, better evidence, and more of it, is needed before the ghost can find its way into the physics and biology textbooks.

What; to begin with, is a ghost? Dictionaries define it as the supposed disembodied spirit, or soul, of a dead person. This

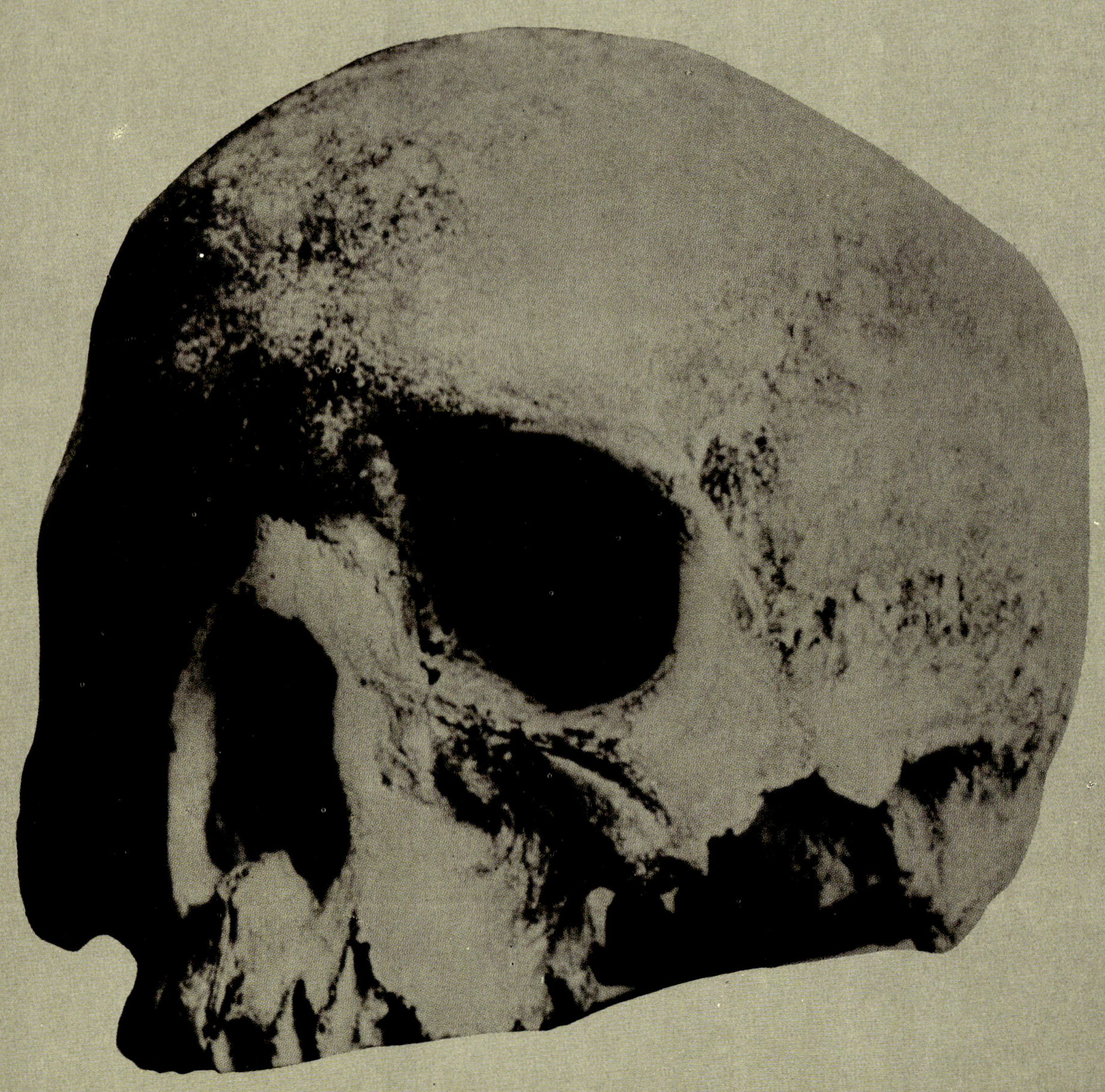

The screaming skull of Bettiscombe Manor in Dorset is said to be that of a West Indian slave who swore his spirit would not rest until he was buried in his African homeland

explanation of the nature of ghosts will not be assumed here, however, for apparitions of living people are frequent. The word 'ghost' has also acquired the sense of a vestige of something, as in 'the ghost of a smile'. Frederic W. H. Myers, a leader of Victorian psychical research, echoed this meaning in his characterisation of a ghost as 'a manifestation of persistent personal energy' – a conclusion he had reached after careful study of a mass of evidence.

A great deal of evidence is available, for seeing or hearing ghostly presences is a very common experience. In 1889 the British Society for Psychical Research, of which Myers was a founder member, embarked upon a large-scale survey of experiences of apparitions, asking the question:

> Have you ever, when believing yourself to be completely awake, had a vivid impression of seeing or being touched by a living being or inanimate object, or of hearing a voice; which impression, so far as you could discover, was not due to any external physical cause?

Almost 10 per cent of the 17,000 people who replied said 'yes'. Later surveys in several other countries confirm this picture.

Isolated appearances of a ghost may be undramatic, but when repeated over a long period become worthy of study. An example is the ghost reported in 1892 by a medical student, Miss R. C. Morton. She wrote:

> I saw the figure of a tall lady dressed in black, standing at the head of the stairs. After a few moments she descended the stairs, and I followed for a short distance, feeling curious what it could be. I had only a small piece of candle, and it suddenly burnt itself out; and being unable to see more, I went to my room.

This ghost lent itself to study. Over the following seven years six people besides Miss Morton saw the ghost, which closely resembled a known former occupant of the house, while about 20 people heard sounds apparently made by it. Sightings followed a regular pattern: the figure would walk downstairs (the resourceful Miss Morton sometimes tied threads across them, but they remained unbroken), enter the drawing-room and stand in the window. Then it would leave the room by the door, walk along the passage and disappear.

Cornering a phantom

Miss Morton, who must have been an exceptionally courageous young woman, made frequent attempts to converse with the ghost, but although it seemed aware of her presence, it never replied. She also tried to touch it, but it always got out of the way. 'On cornering her, as I did once or twice,' she wrote, 'she disappeared.' Miss Morton even tried to 'pounce on it', with the same result.

Once she saw the figure at the usual window and asked her father if he too could

Above: the Brown Lady of Raynham Hall in Norfolk. This ill-defined form was seen by the photographer as well as captured on film

Right: the form of a kneeling monk is said to appear in this picture, taken by a local solicitor in St Nicholas's Church, Arundel, in 1940

The amazing Gladys Hayter

While Gladys Hayter sits in trance, a phantom hand appears, unseen in the darkness but captured in this infra-red photograph

An East London psychic, Gladys Hayter, apparently has the ability to cause phantoms to materialise and living people and inanimate objects to dematerialise and change position, under the gaze of the camera. In 1970 Mrs Hayter, who already practised psychic healing, began photographing strange phenomena with a simple Instamatic camera. Glowing streaks of 'ectoplasm' often appear, emerging from her body. Sometimes her image does not appear in the picture, even though, as she insists, she has not moved. In fact, she claims she is unable to move when in trance during one of these sessions. The picture shown here is one of a number taken by a local photographer, using infra-red film in the near-darkness. The camera on the tripod is Mrs Hayter's.

see it, but he could not. When he walked to the window, the phantom promptly walked round him.

The family's cat took no notice at all of the ghost. The dogs, however, frequently reacted as if they had seen somebody. One would run to the foot of the stairs, wag its tail and jump up as if waiting to be patted, but then back away with its tail between its legs and hide under a sofa. Another dog was often found 'in a state of terror' for no obvious reason. This sensitivity of some animals to supernatural presences has prompted their use as 'ghost-detectors' (see page 68).

In any investigation, it helps to know something of the likely course of events. While the nature of ghosts is still mysterious, their behaviour has been studied in great detail. G. N. M. Tyrell, in his book *Apparitions*, published in 1943, identified four main groups by their pattern of activity.

Below: the kneeling figure in this photograph of the altar of St Mary's Church Woodford, was not seen by the photographer at the time the picture was taken

The first of Tyrrell's groups consists of apparitions that haunt certain places. These, of which Miss Morton's ghost is a typical example, are what are now termed 'place-centred', rather than 'person-centred'. On the whole they do not arouse fear and they sometimes come to be treated as part of the family. They rarely do any harm.

The second category consists of post-mortem apparitions, taking place some time after the death of the person seen, and not related to any particular place or event.

Thirdly, there are crisis cases, in which the apparition is of someone who is undergoing some profound experience at the time (often unknown to the percipient), such as an accident or illness or, of course, death.

Experimental apparitions

The last of Tyrrell's categories is the least-known type of apparition, but perhaps the most intriguing of all – the experimentally induced apparition. The ghost in these cases is not of a dead or dying person but of someone alive and well who has deliberately attempted to make his or her image visible to someone else. Tyrrell found records of 16 successful attempts of this type, and wondered why such an evidently repeatable experiment had been ignored by researchers. It remains a neglected area of study and, although there has been considerable recent study of 'out-of-the-body' experiences, reports of self-induced visibility at a distance remain very rare.

Those ghosts for which evidence is most compelling, and that critical researchers have concluded are genuine, usually show a number of features. Such a ghost obeys the laws of perspective, looking different to different observers; it appears solid; it is visible when viewed in a mirror; and it makes sounds appropriate to its movements – footsteps can be heard, for example. It generally gives the impression of being as real as a

Right: two ghostly forms appear behind the figure of an English lady, Miss Townsend, in the Basilica at Domrémy, in France. The apparitions were unseen by Miss Townsend's companion, Lady Palmer, when she took this photograph during a visit in 1925

Below: another haunting of a holy place. The church in this case is at Newby, in North Yorkshire. Its vicar, the Reverend K. F. Lord, was amazed to find this form on his developed photograph of the altar

living person, if only for a limited period. A sensation of sudden cold may be felt.

The feeling of coldness is also a commonly reported feature of poltergeist cases, but poltergeists are unlike conventional ghosts: they cause physical objects to move, yet they are not seen doing so. Apparitions have been reported in association with poltergeist activity, but we have yet to see one pick up an object and throw it.

When a ghost is seen by only one person, the suspicion arises of hallucination, error or deception – whether practised by the percipient or someone else. But ghosts are often seen by more than one person at the same time, though not necessarily by everybody present. This is often sufficient to rule out the possibility of deception or mistake, but the true nature of the apparition remains unknown. It is not necessarily a disembodied spirit – it could be an 'intersubjective' phenomenon, the joint creation of the percipients' minds.

An apparition may provide some plain evidence of its non-physical nature. It may pass through walls; sometimes it appears and disappears through phantom doors that open and close while 'real' doors stay closed; it may become transparent and fade away.

Nevertheless, these elusive wraiths can apparently be recorded on photographic film. There are many alleged photographs of ghosts, but few are convincing. Fraud has been so prevalent in the field of psychic photography that attention has been diverted

Scene of many hauntings

The ancient manor house at Sandford Orcas, set in an attractive part of Dorset, is the very type of an English haunted house – and it seems to have more than its fair share of ghosts. They include a lady in green; another in red, noted for her punctual appearances at 11.50 a.m. on the stairs; a monk; an Elizabethan lady; a local man who hanged himself in the gatehouse; and Sir Hubert Medlycott, whose family still owns the house. A ghost dog is sometimes seen, and the sound of a phantom spinet can occasionally be heard. The ghost of a footman, 7 feet (2 metres) tall, adds to the problems of the house, for it reputedly takes an improper interest in virgins. It is not, however, often seen nowadays. There are allegedly 14 ghosts in all at the manor – offering a tempting field for the energetic ghost investigator.

from the rare examples that may well be the real thing. One impressive case took place at Raynham Hall, Norfolk, home of the Marquis of Townshend, in 1936. A professional photographer and his assistant were taking photographs of the house. While photographing the staircase, the assistant reported seeing a ghostly figure coming down the stairs. The picture taken at that time, which has been pronounced genuine by photographic experts, does indeed show a misty form. The house has a long history of haunting by a lady in brown, who was seen simultaneously by two witnesses in 1835. Later she was seen by the author Captain Marryat, who ungallantly fired a shotgun at her. Despite this unwelcoming action, she was seen again in 1926 by Lord Townshend and two other witnesses.

Ghostly worshippers

Convincing pictures of ghosts have been taken in churches. In 1940, a local solicitor snapped an unmistakably human form in front of the altar of St Nicholas's church, in Arundel, Sussex. More solid in appearance than the brown lady of Raynham Hall, it was still partly transparent. Some have interpreted it as the figure of a kneeling priest. A similar figure appeared in a photo taken in St Mary's, Woodford, in Northamptonshire, by Gordon Carroll in 1966. Two ghostly priests turned up in the picture of Lady Palmer taken by her friend Miss Townsend in the Basilica of Domrémy, in France.

The prize for technical quality in a ghost photograph must go to the Reverend K. F. Lord of Newby, in Yorkshire, who recorded the presence of a very clear, if somewhat stagey, hollow-eyed spook before his altar.

These are examples of 'place-centred' ghosts. Photographic evidence for 'person-centred' apparitions is more ample. The family photograph albums of the London medium Gladys Hayter contain dozens of colour pictures of inexplicable lights, shadows and – apparently – partly dematerialised living human beings. In 1979 she took a shot of a child in a car, a picture that seems entirely normal except for the fact that, as she has testified, no child was in the car when the picture was taken.

There are no photographs, however, as persuasive as the best eyewitness accounts. Cumulatively, the weight of evidence, of all kinds, suggests that ghosts exist. But, despite a century of intensive research, what they are, and the conditions under which they manifest themselves, are questions that are still awaiting definitive answers. Ghost hunters still face mysteries in plenty.

A serious ghost investigation is long and arduous, and some publicity-conscious authors find it profitable not to be too critical of the cases they retail. What distinguishes a good ghost-hunter from a bad one?

Ghosts true and false

'THE MOST HAUNTED HOUSE in England' was a local inhabitant's description of Borley Rectory, on the Essex-Suffolk border, when he gave directions to a motorist in 1929. The driver was Harry Price, self-styled ghost-hunter and the most energetic and controversial psychical researcher of the century. He found his way to Borley, where he found – or claimed to have found – the ingredients for a series of books, radio broadcasts and newspaper articles that he was to produce for the rest of his life. The case apparently had everything: ringing bells, strange lights, footsteps, flying stones, a skull wrapped in brown paper, mysterious writing on walls, and, of course, a ghost. Local legend had it that the rectory was built on the site of a monastery, from which a monk had unsuccessfully tried to elope with a young lady from a nearby nunnery. Both had been caught and executed, but the nun and the monk (minus his head) and the coach they used were said to be still around. Borley Rectory, Harry Price claimed, was 'the best-authenticated case of haunting in the annals of psychical research.'

This would be welcome news indeed, for surprisingly, although ghosts have been seen over the centuries, very few have ever been investigated thoroughly in order to learn their true nature. But had Price authenticated the Borley hauntings?

Not in the opinion of a team of members of the Society for Psychical Research (SPR), who tore the case to pieces in a devastating report published in 1956. Not only, they claimed, was there no proper evidence for any paranormal occurrences at Borley, but some of the reported phenomena had very probably been caused by Price himself. They quoted one outright accusation of fraud, made by a *Daily Mail* reporter, Charles Sutton, after Price's death:

> Many things happened the night I spent in the famous Borley Rectory with Harry Price and one of his colleagues, including one uncomfortable moment when a large pebble hit me on the head.
>
> After much noisy 'phenomena' I seized Harry and found his pockets full of bricks and pebbles. This was one 'phenomenon' he could not explain, so I rushed to the nearest village to 'phone the *Daily Mail* with my story, but after a conference with the lawyer my story was killed.

Even some of Price's fellow investigators concluded that he was more interested in a good story than in the truth of the case. A

A brick flung through the air at the site of the ruined Borley Rectory is captured on film by a *Life* magazine photographer. Harry Price, who was present at the time, later cited this picture as photographic evidence of poltergeist activity at Borley – without mentioning the workman who was demolishing a nearby wall when the picture was taken

typical example of this was given by a *Life* magazine reporter, Cynthia Ledsham, who visited Borley with Price and a photographer in 1944. The rectory, which had burned down in 1939, was being demolished. The photographer took a distant shot of the ruins, which showed a brick flying through the air. Price later claimed that this could be 'the first photograph ever taken of a poltergeist projectile in flight'. However, the reporter later admitted to the SPR investigators that while the picture was being taken a workman was dismantling a wall nearby, throwing bricks at regular intervals. She accused Price of 'the most bare-faced hocus pocus'.

Price's account of the haunting was demolished as surely as the building itself. The rectory had not been built on the site of a monastery after all. The 'nun' who had been spotted by a newspaper reporter 'flitting about in the gloom' was in fact the maid, a lively girl who later admitted to having carried out a spot of poltergeist activity herself. One former occupant of the rectory declared it to have been haunted by no more than 'rats and local superstition'. Another, the source of a great deal of the anecdotal material (which Price himself privately admitted to not believing), turned out to have lived previously near Amherst in Nova Scotia, scene of a well-publicised 19th-century haunting with many remarkable similarities to the alleged happenings at Borley. And so the indictment continues through 180 pages of a special issue of the SPR's *Proceedings* wholly devoted to an exposé of Price's bold claims.

In Trevor H. Hall's *Search for Harry Price* (1948), the 'ghost-hunter extraordinary' is depicted as a publicity-seeking charlatan and an unscrupulous liar. Although argument was still raging in 1980 in the pages of the SPR's *Journal* over both the facts of the Borley case and the integrity of its investigator-publicist, it cannot be claimed that Price made any useful contribution at all to our understanding of ghosts, or that there is any reason to believe a word of what he wrote about Borley.

Shock, horror, thrills

One moral of this lamentable episode seems to be that it is all too easy, and profitable, to offer the public what it wants – shock, horror and occult thrills. It is much more difficult and costly to do the painstaking work of a good investigator. The late Jay Anson, who scripted the film based on the novel *The exorcist*, made an estimated £3 million from his book *The Amityville horror*, but he had no first-hand experience of this case whatsoever. A researcher who followed up the case, Dr Stephen Kaplan, dismissed the book as 'mostly fiction'. Another writer who investigated the story, Melvin Harris, has written that 'there is plenty of evidence which shows unambiguously that the Amityville story is a gross fabrication'.

How, then, should ghosts be hunted? In an ideal world, funds, personnel and equipment would be available for an enquiry as thoroughly conducted as a police murder

Right: wreckage scattered over Florida swampland after the crash of Eastern Airlines' flight 401 on 29 December 1972, with two of the crew who died. The ghosts of the pilot, Bob Loft (centre), and the second officer, Don Repo (below), were later seen on other Eastern Airlines Tri-Star flights (inset)

A television special

In 1964 Anglia Television filmed a documentary at an allegedly haunted 16th-century manor house, Morley Old Hall in Norfolk. Anthony D. Cornell (below left) demonstrated how a ghost-hunter worked. After a night's investigation, he was interviewed in the room where the ghost was said to have appeared. He concluded there was little evidence for the haunting.

Five people contacted the television company to say that they had seen a 'hooded monk' standing between Cornell and the interviewer, Michael Robson. Although Robson could see nothing when he re-ran the film, he decided to broadcast it again. Viewers were asked to write in if they saw anything odd.

Twenty-seven viewers wrote in. Fifteen said they had seen a monk or priest; one said it was a lady in a mantilla; one said it was a hooded skull.

When some of the relevant frames were enlarged, certain markings were at last seen that corresponded with drawings sent in by viewers. They proved to be due to dampness on the stonework.

As Anthony Cornell commented, the case was of interest to psychical researchers. The dim lighting of the television screen and the 'atmosphere' engendered by the rest of the film favoured 'spectral' appearances. Secondly, an impressive number of witnesses sited the 'figure' exactly at the spot where a physical cause was later found. Lastly, although the markings were vague, many of the witnesses were in substantial agreement about the 'figure' they saw.

hunt, or as research into subatomic particles or the mating habits of cockroaches. But they are not available, and the work is left to individual investigators, many of whom understandably make a living by writing about their experiences. The best to be hoped for is that such individuals will record as much first-hand evidence as they can, as soon as possible after the event.

While the perfect ghost investigation has yet to be recorded, at least two cases of the 1970s were researched and written up in considerable detail. One consisted of a series of apparitions on board several jumbo jets of an American airline.

Airborne apparitions

An Eastern Airlines Tri-Star, flight 401, crashed in December 1972 in a Florida swamp, killing 101 people. The ghosts of the pilot, Bob Loft, and his flight engineer, Don Repo, were seen on more than twenty occasions by crew members of other Eastern Tri-Stars, especially those that had been fitted with salvaged parts of the crashed plane. The apparitions were invariably described as wholly lifelike. They were reported both by men and women who had known Loft and Repo and by others who had not, but who recognised them later from photographs. The haunting became well-known among people in the airline community, and an account of it even appeared in the newsletter of the US Flight Safety Foundation, in 1974.

An author, John G. Fuller, made thorough investigations of the case with the help of several airline personnel. They produced a mass of compelling testimony, including claims that log books recording apparitions had been withdrawn and crew members reporting them had been threatened with a visit to the company psychiatrist. Moreover, a seance was eventually held in the presence of Repo's widow at which evidence was produced that satisfied her of her husband's continuing existence. This would be a near-perfect case if the airline had co-operated but, perhaps understandably, it did not.

It is to be hoped that future ghosts will be as visible and informative as Loft and Repo, and that future hunters will be as determined as the investigators of this famous case. Ghost-hunting, says Andrew Green, himself an expert in the art, 'enlarges the field of knowledge, which is in itself a valid reason for any pursuit.' But for the dedicated ghost-hunter, the sheer fascination of the chase is a sufficient spur.

A ghost hunter's guide

Resourcefulness and skill are required to carry out an investigation of ghostly apparitions. This chapter describes how a good ghost hunter tests the authenticity of a haunting

FINDING A GHOST worthy of investigation is not too difficult. It is rather like looking for a flat: just as home hunters can go to an agency, look in the papers, and 'ask around', so ghost hunters can seek information from official organisations, from the specialised press and from friends and work-mates.

The first step for the would-be ghost hunter is to join a parapsychological organisation which exist in most countries. In Britain there is the Society for Psychical Research (SPR). It was founded in 1882 'to examine without prejudice or prepossession and in a scientific spirit those faculties of man, real or supposed, which appear to be inexplicable on any generally recognised hypothesis.' The SPR *Journal* is published regularly; its *Proceedings*, containing full reports and more technical articles, appears irregularly. It holds regular meetings and annual international conferences; and it offers its members, of which there are more than a thousand, the use of its unique library. It holds no corporate views, and its membership includes men and women with or without qualifications or religious convictions. Although ghosts are only one of many areas of research that come within its scope, the majority of Britain's serious ghost hunters have been, or are, members.

Above: the ghost hunter's dream come true – a meeting face-to-face with an apparition. However, this eminent investigator, the physicist Sir William Crookes, is generally thought to have been duped. The medium responsible for the 'materialisation' – Florence Cook, here apparently recumbent on the floor – bore a remarkable physical resemblance to the 'spirit', Katie King

The British weekly *Psychic News* is also an excellent source of new case material. Any good public library will have a number of books by such experienced ghost hunters as Andrew Green, Peter Underwood, Joan Forman and Andrew Mackenzie, many of which give the addresses of places with a well-established history of haunting. *Ghost-hunting, a practical guide* (1973) by Andrew Green is a particularly clear and concise work for beginners seeking a general introduction to the subject. The SPR's *Notes for investigators of spontaneous cases* are also recommended.

Finally, one can attempt to find a case by word-of-mouth contact. Since about one person in ten has had some kind of paranormal experience, it is more than likely that in an average office or factory there is somebody who has seen a ghost or knows someone who has.

Preliminary assessment

When a case has been found, the first thing to do is to make sure that there is enough firm evidence to make it worth investigating. The criteria for assessing evidence are much the same as in a criminal enquiry, and a study of police methods is useful to the ghost hunter. The following notes may sound somewhat obvious, but it is amazing how often research has been hampered because they have not been observed in the past.

Witnesses' descriptions must be recorded, in writing or, preferably, on tape. The place and date, both of the incident described and of the statement, should be included. Written statements should be signed.

Second-hand accounts are almost never of value. First-hand accounts of a single event by a single witness are virtually impossible to verify and, though they are worth recording, they are seldom worth following up, since further occurrences are unlikely.

If there are several witnesses, they should be interviewed separately. Questioning should be deferred until the statements have been obtained, in order not to put ideas into the witnesses' heads. Questioning will almost certainly be necessary, however, to make up deficiencies in the statements. The aim should be to arrive at as full an account as possible of the circumstances of the incident:

Above: Joan Forman has written valuable guides to the haunted places of East Anglia and southern England

Above right: the Society for Psychical Research plots cases of hauntings on this map, and maintains copious files concerning them

Below right: photographic evidence of a haunting, obtained by a budding ghost hunter. Andrew Green, then a 15-year-old boy, walked around this empty and reputedly haunted house in 1944. When he left, he took this photograph. When it was developed he was amazed to see the figure at the upper window. A murder and no fewer than 20 suicides took place here. It has been suggested that the figure is an apparition of Ann Hinchfield, who jumped from the tower in 1886, when she was 12 years old

Below: Andrew Green, today a noted researcher and author on parapsychology

time and place, the witnesses' activities and states of mind immediately before and during it, the physical layout of the scene, the positions of other people, independent confirming evidence – broken or displaced objects, for example – and any similar experiences that the witnesses may have had.

The occasional trick question can be useful. For example: 'Mrs Smith says the ghost was wearing a green hat. Are you *sure* it was bare-headed?' If the witness suddenly 'remembers' the green hat (which Mrs Smith did not mention) the hunter is dealing with an unreliable witness.

The witnesses should be interviewed on more than one occasion. Their stories may develop from one telling to the next; if so, it is necessary to judge whether this is really due to an increased recall, or to continuing inventiveness.

On the basis of these preliminary enquiries, which should be routine for any ghost report, the ghost hunter must judge whether a serious follow-up investigation is justified. Ideally, detailed and consistent reports will be provided by several witnesses, of good local reputations and no apparent motives for deceit (such as a council tenant's desire for a better house).

If more thorough research is undertaken, possible natural causes for the reported incident must first be sought. Ghostly noises are often made by such everyday agencies as the wind, water pipes, windows or ornaments vibrating in resonance with passing traffic, animals and so on. In one case a family was haunted by no more than rats, pushing apples stored in a loft down a cavity wall.

A superficial search for such a cause has a good chance of finding such a mundane explanation, but the variety of possible misleading occurrences is so great that little can

usefully be said here as guidance. The investigator must be sceptical of the easy paranormal explanations that suggest themselves, and imaginative in devising commonplace (but possibly far from obvious) causes that can be tested; he or she must aim to be a Sherlock Holmes of psychic detection, in fact.

A thorough investigation of the phenomena needs equipment (see box), patience and an acceptance of the likelihood of disappointment. If the occurrences are person-centred, there are great difficulties. It is rarely practicable to keep someone under continuous observation for long periods – let alone restrain their movements while apparent ghost activity is under way. There is

The well-equipped investigator

If the frequency of appearances is sufficient to justify lying in wait for a ghost, there is no end of material that might be useful to the investigator. The area being observed can be sealed off from human access by putting masking tape along the edges of doors and windows. Threads stretched across the ghost's route and scattered chalk powder will reveal a human presence. Fluorescent powder can also be scattered in suitable places – if it is picked up on the person of some occupant of the house, it will reveal itself when ultra-violet light is shone on it. Capacitance switches can be purchased, which will actuate cameras and tape recorders at the approach of a human being or animal. Tape recordings should be made in stereo if possible, and if an area can be surveyed with more than one tripod-mounted camera, so much the better. The 'fastest' (most sensitive) films available are black and white, and these can also be 'pushed' considerably in developing, in order to bring out more detail. If, however, it is planned to use flash, there is no reason why colour film should not be used. Since the space to be covered is usually confined, a short-focus (wide-angle) lens is valuable. A motor-drive attachment permits a sequence of photographs to be taken rapidly. Such obvious items as note-books, pens, torch, luminous watch and a simple tool-kit should also not be omitted from the equipment list.

also the problem that people's feelings will be ruffled if they come to believe that they are being suspected of fraud.

On the other hand, ghostly phenomena, like some other paranormal events, may happen more predictably in the presence of certain people, and offer the opportunity of detailed study. Many mediums have claimed that it is possible to materialise a spirit. Past studies of such events, such as those carried out by the eminent physicist William Crookes in 1874, are still surrounded by controversy. Yet there remains a substantial body of evidence that certain mediums, such as the late Alec Harris, are able to cause such phenomena. It is a sad fact of the history of ghost hunting that few people have ever made a serious attempt to examine this subject properly. There are great opportunities for the ghost hunter here.

The late Alec Harris, one of those mediums who can reputedly materialise spirits – an ability that may be related to some 'ordinary' hauntings

Setting up a team

Establishing the genuineness of a case is very much a matter of personal judgement, and since this is highly fallible, it is always a good idea for more than one person to study a given case. Unless the investigator is a qualified psychologist, physicist and chartered surveyor combined, he will need help from specialists. Furthermore, if an investigation team can be set up, it may be possible to keep the site under constant observation.

Ghost hunters will naturally want to see reported apparitions for themselves. They will almost certainly be disappointed. Perhaps ghosts will appear to order when we know more about the conditions they require; in the meantime, the more evidence that can be recorded about such conditions, the better for paranormal research.

Whatever the results of an investigation – whether it is called off at an early stage, ends inconclusively, or ends in a finding of fraud, misinterpretation or the genuinely paranormal – a report should be filed with the ASPR. In addition to its intrinsic interest it may gain significance in the future should it be studied in relation to other cases, or should developments take place in the same case.

Where ghostly activities genuinely seem to be taking place, the question of getting rid of them may arise. If the ghost is not doing any harm, there is no need to do anything. In fact, it can be very good for trade in a pub or hotel (one of the motives for deceit that the ghost hunter must bear in mind).

But not all ghosts are harmless. The witnesses can be extremely frightened, and the phenomena can disrupt family life – or even, as in some recent cases, factory and office life. How can they be got rid of? There is no easy answer, but certain methods have been tried, with uneven success.

The best-known of these is exorcism. At the risk of oversimplifying this emotive and controversial subject, it can be said that it may be effective if the victim believes it will be. But it can also have dangerous side-effects, and in at least four well-reported cases of the 1970s, involving both Roman Catholics and Protestants, its use resulted in death.

A somewhat safer and less sensational way to combat an invisible agency is prayer. Canon J. D. Pearce-Higgins, former Vice-Provost of Southwark Cathedral, claims to have 'cleared' more than a hundred houses of 'unwanted visitors', by first identifying the entities with the help of a medium, and then persuading them to depart.

Ghosts will doubtless continue to provide entertainment in the newspapers and on the screen, and ghost hunters will continue to be regarded by some as harmless cranks. Yet the subject is a serious one, of tremendous potential significance. Once fully understood, it will vastly extend our knowledge both of the human mind and of matter. But it will not be understood unless far more people take it more seriously and investigate it more thoroughly. And the more amateur ghost hunters there are, collecting more and better evidence and forcing it upon the attention of scientists, the sooner this will happen.

Old soldiers never die

Phantoms are not always the lonely beings of the traditional ghost story; sometimes, especially in damp weather, they appear in large numbers, re-enacting old battles

THE BATTLE OF NASEBY, in Northamptonshire, England, was fought on 14 June 1645. One of the major engagements of the English Civil War, it ended in the rout of the Royalist forces by the Parliamentary armies. But it seems to have been fought not once, but repeatedly – to have been 'replayed' annually for about a century afterwards. Local villagers would congregate on a nearby hill to witness the re-enactment of the fight. The watchers heard cannonfire and saw men fighting and falling, banners flying and cavalry charging; they even heard the screams and groans of the wounded. Yet all this was enacted in the sky above the battlefield.

We are accustomed to think of ghosts as single apparitions, appearing one at a time to one or two observers. But some records exist of large-scale hauntings – of phantoms appearing *en masse*, engaged in collective activity. They are often refighting some historic battle, as in the case above.

Another important engagement of the Civil War, the battle of Marston Moor, near York, is re-enacted from time to time, according to a local legend. The most favourable weather for the occurrence of the apparition is said to be fog, even though the original battle of 1644 was fought in midsummer.

Yet another Civil War battle fought over again by phantoms was the battle of Edgehill (1642). Only a few days after the battle, there were reports of apparitions of soldiers, cavalry and phantom scenery – all appearing in the sky over the battlefield. King Charles sent a number of army officers from Oxford to the site – and they witnessed the events, swearing statements to that effect (see page 66).

Writer Joan Forman experienced the terror of a long-past battle herself, when travelling in Scotland some years ago. She had chosen to stay in Selkirk, because it is a good centre for touring and because she was interested in the career of James Graham, the first

An army sleeps on the eve of battle, while phantom warfare rages in the skies above. The apparition may be an anticipation of the bloodshed to come, or a re-enactment of some past engagement. Stories of 'armies in the sky' seen over battlefields are numerous – suggesting that the strenuous exertion and intense emotion of combat are somehow favourable to psychic phenomena

movement and, in spite of heroic charges by the Royalist leader and his cavalry, had slowly driven them back until they were pinned beneath the mass of Minchmoor.

At this point in the narrative, Forman looked over the edge of the Newark courtyard and without warning was engulfed in a feeling of frantic misery and desperation. There was a sensation of turmoil, of many people struggling to escape and being forced back – not against the far side of the valley but right underneath the walls of the castle itself. She stood there for a few minutes, but the sense of furious and desperate fighting was unbearable. She moved away.

As she did so, she said that she believed Montrose's men had been massacred on this side of the valley and not on the other. The guide shook his head. 'Oh, no,' he said, 'I'm sure you're wrong. It is acknowledged that they died on the farther side.' She did not pursue the matter.

Then, as they walked away from that miserable place above the escarpment, Forman

Marquis of Montrose. This great cavalier leader had been Charles I's chief supporter in Scotland – his Captain-General. He had fought the Covenanting forces, which sided with the English Parliament. He had spectacular gifts as a soldier, and in 1644 led his armies in some brilliant forced marches across the mountains to achieve equally extraordinary victories over the King's enemies.

But towards the end of that year Montrose found that his luck began to run out. In attempting to lead his small army away from a much larger force of the enemy, led by General David Leslie, Montrose headed for Philiphaugh, a small plateau near Selkirk, where the Glen of Yarrow meets that of Ettrick, and camped there.

But Leslie was almost upon them. Leslie's army of 6000 men fell on Montrose's force of 700. The Royalists were driven from one end of the valley to the other before they were penned in and cut down. The *annus mirabilis* of Montrose ended in the massacre of his men.

Local tradition has it that the Royalists were pinned down on the side of the valley that lies beneath Minchmoor. On the opposite side of the valley lay a castle known as Newark, perched on an escarpment above the battlefield. It was also said that, although General Leslie offered quarter to those Royalists who surrendered, many of the men and their camp followers were slaughtered after the battle.

Forman already knew of the battle, but not its details, and so she was glad when a knowledgeable Selkirk historian offered to guide her around the site. They found the ruins of the old Newark keep, isolated in its wild and beautiful valley, and entered the remains of the old courtyard. The guide began to describe the battle to her: how Leslie had caught Montrose's small force in a pincer

Top: a crucial battle of the English Civil War is marked by this monument at Naseby, Northamptonshire. Local people saw phantom re-enactments of it during the following 100 years

Above: Oliver Cromwell at the battle of Marston Moor, in Yorkshire. Apparitions of this battle are alleged to occur even today

Right: James Graham, first Marquis of Montrose, led a small Royalist force that was massacred at Philiphaugh, Scotland. Over 300 years later, the terror of the event was apparently experienced by the author while visiting the site

was again immersed in a wave of terror and anguish, now coming from the courtyard itself. This time the feeling of fear and wretched despair were overwhelming: for a few seconds she was unable to move. The air seemed filled with cries of anguish, though she knew she was hearing nothing with the ear.

'It's here,' she said. 'They killed them here in this very courtyard. Where I am standing, and over there by the wall. They must have executed a whole lot of people in this very place.'

The Selkirk man was silent, visibly upset. Finally he said: 'There were people killed later, I think. Leslie went back on his promise; some of the non-combatants – women and boys – were killed, and afterwards some of the men. But I don't think that it was here.'

She said no more, but the misery of the place was heavy and she was glad to go from it.

The kindly historian telephoned the following day and said that the curious episode had so impressed him that he had further investigated the local records. 'It seems you may be right and tradition wrong,' he said. 'There's a contemporary record that refers to the castle side of the valley as being the scene of the final massacre, and that would make it right under the place where we stood. What's more, there seems to be some justification for thinking executions did take place in the castle bailey after the battle.'

Some of Forman's ancestors belonged to the Graham clan and may have fought at Philiphaugh with their chief, Graham of Montrose. Could this fact have helped to make her a particularly sensitive 'receiver' for this strange experience?

Sounds of clashing metal

A further example of 'participation' in a past battle occurred in Windsor in the early 1970s. A house owned by Mr and Mrs Wakefield-Smith was apparently haunted by a man in a dark cloak, and they felt the atmosphere of the place to be unhappy. The garden, however, proved to be an equally interesting site. On one occasion when the owners had walked to the end of it, they suddenly seemed to be in an area of great heat and noise. Both husband and wife felt they were in the middle of a battle, for all around them were the sounds of clashing metal, like swords striking armour. There was a sensation of frenzied activity on all sides. Yet as suddenly as it began the phenomenon ended, and the garden was its usual tranquil self.

Although the Wakefield-Smiths' description of the ghosts suggests the Civil War period, the only battle referred to by local tradition was of a much earlier date, and was fought between Romans and Britons. It seems likely that this is what the couple encountered.

The great heat associated with the occurrence is interesting. Hauntings are generally associated with a fall in temperature, and this did indeed accompany the appearances of the ghost in the house. Was the experience of the battle a haunting, then, or some quite different phenomenon?

Not all large-scale manifestations relate to battles. The night-time activity seen by Dr and Mrs White at the beginning of January, 1969 on the Isle of Wight did not seem to have anything to do with war. Miss Edith Olivier, a Wiltshire author, was involved in a similar event during the First World War. She was driving towards the great Avebury Ring of standing stones as dusk was falling. As she came within sight of the circle she saw what she thought was an entire fair erected around and among the stones; she could hear music and see the lights of the booths. But as she drew level she found that the circle was empty, and there was no sound but that of the wind sighing among the great monoliths. Later Miss Olivier's enquiries revealed that fairs had been held at this spot in the past, but it had been at least 50 years since the last.

Frequently, communities that have lived

Above: Newark Castle, seen across the valley that was the scene of James Graham's defeat. The conventional opinion of historians is that Graham's men were trapped on the opposite side of the valley – behind the camera's viewpoint. But Joan Forman's experience while visiting the castle – apparently a 'replay' of the emotions of the battle – convinced her that the battle ended beneath the castle walls

Left: the keep of Newark Castle, from the courtyard. Here Forman experienced, for the second time, the sensation of being engulfed in the anguish of many people. Her belief that the massacre that followed the battle had taken place in the courtyard proved to be supported by independent historical evidence – as did her intuition about the battle itself

by an inflexible timetable reappear regularly in apparitional form for many years after their earthly disappearance. Thus groups of monks and nuns, accustomed to process and attend prayer at set times of the day and night, may be seen and heard repeating the same pattern centuries later. Such stories are numerous throughout Britain. At Hinxworth Place, near Baldock in Hertfordshire, processions of monks have been seen to come through a wall, apparently on their way to or from their worship through a doorway long bricked up.

Occasionally an entire church congregation is seen, as at Dallington, Northamptonshire, in 1907. Two schoolgirls visited a country church at the end of a walk. One, a local girl, entered the church first but came out again in a great hurry. Her companion, a visitor to the area, was intrigued and went into the building. The place seemed full of kneeling people, though they appeared, she afterwards said, 'to be made of a substance similar to soap bubbles'. There seem to be no other reports of similar apparitions at this site, and there is no indication of the period to which the ghostly worshippers belonged.

Yet another instance of a group apparition was reported from Wiltshire, where a detachment of Roman soldiers was said to march along the old road beyond Oldbury Camp. A shepherd who sighted the band on one occasion gave this description of them: 'Men with beards, wearing skirts and big helmets with hair on the top. And a girt bird on a pole a' front on 'em.' A fair, if somewhat rustic, description of a Roman column, carrying its eagle insignia at its head.

Soldiers, in small groups or whole armies, in war or peace, seem to supply the bulk of mass-phantom phenomena. One of the most interesting cases is that of Major A. D. McDonagh, an officer serving in the Indian Army on the North-West Frontier.

Above: Hinxworth Place, in Hertfordshire, is one of the many places in England where a ghostly religious ritual is said to occur: a procession of monks appears through a wall

Below: a typically English church, at Dallington, in Northamptonshire. The ghostly congregation seen briefly in 1907 was more insubstantial – seemingly made of 'soap bubbles'

On one occasion the Major rode along a range of hills close to the River Indus. He eventually reached a ridge from which he could see across a wide horseshoe-shaped valley, which was heavily wooded. As he gazed down onto it, he abruptly found himself in a large group of soldiers, apparently from ancient Greek times, busy with the usual duties of a military encampment. He saw three altars, and noticed a group of men beyond them, at the head of the valley, gathered around some object. McDonagh could not see what was holding their attention until he walked across. Then he perceived a dressed stone slab with a newly cut inscription. The language was Greek, of which in ordinary life he had no knowledge. However, he found himself able to read and understand what was written here: the inscription seemed to relate to the death of one of the generals of Alexander the Great. He felt, too, a marked sensation of sorrow among the men with whom he stood.

Evidence in stone

Abruptly, the experience ended. Major McDonagh found himself back on the ridge, looking down into the valley, vividly aware of what he had just experienced.

Later he returned with Indian labourers to explore the area thoroughly. He found the place heavily overgrown with jungle vegetation and the men had to hack their way through to the head of the valley in which he had seen the inscribed rock. When eventually they reached it and cleared away the vegetation, they found a partially dressed rock surface with some traces of Greek lettering upon it, though the inscription was

Left: Oldbury Camp, an Iron Age earthwork in Wiltshire, apparently occupied by the Romans when they subdued Britain. A detachment of Roman soldiers is said still to march along the line of the old Roman road nearby

Below: Alexander the Great, (in a crown) before a Hindu idol, following his crossing of the Indus river in 326 BC. The painting is from a 15th-century Persian manuscript. A British officer, Major McDonagh, who had been riding near the river, suddenly found himself in the midst of this army. For an extended period he watched the men, apparently in mourning for one of their generals

badly eroded and defaced. McDonagh had no doubt, however, that this was the memorial he had seen earlier. The valley proved to be the site of one of the camps of Alexander before he forded the Indus in 326 BC.

This account is a particularly interesting example of a mass-phantom appearance. The distance in time between the original episode and its modern 'repeat' was over 2000 years – an exceptional period in these cases. Furthermore, the subject of the experience participated in the events he witnessed – moving around to get a view of the things he wanted to see, and finding himself able to understand a language normally unknown to him.

The idea of reincarnation suggests itself in cases like these. Was Major McDonagh a solider in Alexander's army in some former life? Or did he merely 'pick up' the sensations of the troop who had stood by the rock with its inscription to the dead general?

Occurrences of this nature are too rare to provide much evidence. However, appearances of phantoms *en masse* are not. There are at least two possible explanations of these. They may involve the *reproduction* of the sights and sounds of the original event – possibly because information stored by the physical surroundings is, in favourable conditions, 'retransmitted' to create the impression in the minds of certain specially sensitive witnesses that they are actually observing the original events. Alternatively, they may be true timeslips, in which past and present, or present and future, coexist temporarily. However, this process too might be triggered by the mind of the witness, interacting with information registered by the physical surroundings.

Ghosts on the march

Sometimes crowds of phantom figures appear, acting out events long past – or, occasionally, in the future. But why are so many mass phantom cases usually linked with emotional happenings?

THE OCCASIONAL SIGHTINGS of mass apparitions fall into a shadowy area in which it is difficult to distinguish timeslips from hauntings. The large-scale noise and activity, involving many phantom individuals at one time, and the sense of being overwhelmed by associated emotions, suggest that the subject has been plunged into events in some other era. On the other hand, the co-presence of familiar features of the everyday world suggests that it is the phantoms who have strayed into the wrong time.

A high proportion of mass phantom appearances relate to military activity. If they are a 'recording' of historical events, and if such recording is especially likely to occur in the presence of increased mental and emotional stress – and the evidence points in this direction – then it is not surprising that battles should figure so strongly among apparitions.

Weather conditions also seem to be important. Grey, overcast skies, mist or fog seem to be conducive to paranormal effects. One such case was reported by Mrs E. W. Reeves, of Holme Hale, Norfolk, England.

Mrs Reeves and her husband visited friends some miles away on the evening in question and returned home at about 2.30 a.m. The Moon was shining and there were patches of mist when Mrs Reeves got out of the car to open the garage doors for her husband. She heard shouting in the near distance and she drew her husband's attention to it, saying that she thought someone might be in need of help. Mr Reeves, however, who had not yet heard any sound, considered 2.30 in the morning to be an unlikely time for anyone to be needing assistance.

In the next moment the shouting was taken up by other voices, and now Mr Reeves also heard it. The clamour was accompanied by the sound of many running feet. Mr Reeves remarked that the sound seemed to be coming from the far side of a bridge a few hundred yards away. Disturbed and curious, the couple moved into the roadway for a better view. Nothing was to be seen, but the noises continued, presently augmented by the sounds of galloping horses.

The thought that anything paranormal was happening did not occur to the couple. They assumed that the horses they could hear belonged to a neighbouring farmer and they were concerned about stopping their flight. The galloping and shouting drew nearer, but the village street remained as empty of anything visible as when they had first left the car.

The sounds were now so loud that whatever was causing them appeared to be all around the couple, 'milling around us and

Above: a battle in the sky over Verviers, Belgium, in June 1815 – within a month of the battle of Waterloo, some 70 miles (110 kilometres) away. It was explained away as a mirage – yet mirages occur simultaneously with the events that cause them

Left: the rebellion of Robert Ket in 1549 may have been 'witnessed' over 400 years later. After the defeat of Ket – here seen denouncing a landowner – some of the rebels fled through the village of Holme Hale, where a phantom battle was heard in the 20th century

around the Red Lion forecourt opposite our house'. There were further sounds, 'of sticks hitting swords. It was like listening to a Robin Hood film fight.'

By now both husband and wife were bewildered, and shrank against the wall of their house, trying to evade whatever it was that was crashing around them. Presently the commotion shifted away from where they stood, into a field located next to the inn. Finally the noises moved up the hill beyond and faded into the distance. After that, according to Mrs Reeves, all the dogs in the village began to howl simultaneously, and continued to do so for several minutes.

The BBC later investigated this incident for a television programme called *Timeslips*. Their research revealed that, although no pitched battle in the neighbourhood of Holme Hale was on record, there were several likely candidates for the disturbance experienced by Mr and Mrs Reeves. The district was twice pillaged by the Danes in the 11th century; a series of riots against the enclosure of common lands occurred in the 1530s; there was further rioting during Ket's Rebellion in 1549, in which some of the rebels fled from Castle Rising to Watton, pursuing a line of retreat passing directly through Holme Hale. Certainly the rebel forces had a camp at Hingham, a short distance away, which was attacked by the troops of Sir Edmund Knyvett. The battle appears to have been fought with staves on one side and swords on the other, suggesting peasants facing organised troops. Ket's rising would appear to fit the facts of the case.

A well-documented sighting was reported by Dr James McHarg in the *Journal* of the Society for Psychical Research for December 1978. The incident concerned a Miss Smith, to whom the experience occurred in January 1950. She was walking home to the village of Letham in Angus, Scotland, after spending the evening at a friend's house. She had been driving back but her car had skidded on the icy road and into a ditch. She had therefore decided to walk the remaining 8 miles (13 kilometres).

She was about half a mile (800 metres) from her home village when the apparition began. It continued until she reached the houses, the whole experience lasting about 12 minutes. She must have been exceedingly

Below: Viking raiders may have been involved in the event that was acted out in the Holme Hale apparition. Vikings occupied large areas of Britain from the 8th to the 11th century. It was towards the end of this period that Holme Hale was twice pillaged by Danish marauders

tired at this time, for she had been carrying her small dog for the last part of the journey.

The experience began as she crested a rise that in daylight would have given her a view of Dunnichen Hill. Now, with the time nearing 2 a.m., she saw moving torches in the distance ahead of her. As she continued her journey, she followed a left-hand turning that brought the torches onto her right. Still farther down the road on her right, she saw other figures carrying torches. There were figures even closer to her, however, in a field about 50 yards (45 metres) distant. Miss Smith felt that she had stumbled upon some activity that was already in progress when she arrived.

The area that Miss Smith was traversing was the site of an ancient and now vanished loch, known as Nechtanesmere, a name given to it by the English rather than the Scots. It had been the scene of a battle in May 685. The Northumbrians, captained by their king, Egfrith, were defeated here by the Picts under their king Brude mac Beli, and the Northumbrian chief was killed. After falling into an ambush Egfrith's army was apparently routed, and the most desperate fighting seems to have taken place near the shores of the old loch.

This was the area crossed by Miss Smith, and although the loch waters had long been replaced by dry land, she apparently knew that a lake had once existed there, for her account referred to figures 'quite obviously skirting the mere'. She concluded that they were searching for their dead, for she noticed one person in particular turning over body after body and scrutinising each. The corpses also must therefore have been visible.

Miss Smith gave an excellent description of the dress worn by the figures. She saw

Above: the area bordering the site of a vanished loch, Nechtanesmere, which was traversed by phantom figures on a January night in 1950. Miss E.F. Smith watched them for about 12 minutes as the torch-carrying men apparently searched among corpses for their own dead, slain in battle. The battle of Nechtanesmere, fought in 685, resulted in the defeat of Egfrith, king of the Northumbrians, by the Pictish king Brude mac Beli

Right: a Pictish warrior, carved on a stone among animals and fish. His dress resembles that of the figures seen by Miss Smith: a tunic with a rolled hem and collar, and tights

'dark tights' and 'a sort of overall with a roll-collar'. There was a roll at the bottom of the tunic. The headgear seemed to be a flattish rolled cap, 'excellent for carrying things on the head with'. The torches were very long and made of a bright red material.

Dr McHarg obtained these details directly from Miss Smith in September 1971 and thoroughly investigated the background to her experience. He found that torches in Scotland were once made from the resinous roots of the Scots fir, which are reddish in colour, and would have been notable for their length. The costume description, too, is borne out by the dress of a figure of a Pictish warrior incised in stone at Golspie.

All in all, this is an impressive apparition. It has marked parallels with that experienced by Dr and Mrs White on the Isle of Wight in the winter of 1969. Both experiences occurred in January, though the weather was different: on the Isle of Wight it was cold, with brilliant moonlight and towering cloud masses, while at Nechtanesmere it was cold and wet after a snowfall that had been followed by rain. In each case the onset of the

Flight into the future

Phantoms *en masse* are frequently seen in the air – but in one notable case an apparition on the ground was viewed from the air. Air Marshal Sir Victor Goddard told how in 1934 he had been flying a Hawker Hart bomber (left) over Scotland in mist and rain. He flew lower, looking for an abandoned airfield, Drem, as a landmark. He found it – apparently bathed in sunlight, and fully operational. Yellow aircraft were on the tarmac, being serviced by technicians in blue overalls. No one paid any attention to Goddard as he flew low overhead and then resumed his journey. It was only several years later that the meaning of what he had seen became clear to him. In 1938 Drem was put back into service as a flight training station. Trainer aircraft were for the first time painted yellow and ground crew were issued with a new style of uniform – coloured blue. Goddard believed he had glimpsed Drem airfield as it was to be.

vision took place as the parties crested a hill. Both apparitions featured the same type of scene: searching figures carrying lighted torches. It seems likely that they were engaged on the same mission in both cases – a search for the dead after a battle, in order to bury them. The differences in costume in the two cases are explicable by the differences in locality and, presumably, in the dates of the original events.

Action replay

For there seems little doubt that what was seen was in both cases some historical event – a record of a large-scale undertaking in the distant past. The most likely 'source' event is a battle, and the details of the battle of Nechtanesmere are sufficiently well-known to make its correspondence with Miss Smith's vision apparent. The reality behind the Whites' experience must remain speculative, for the Isle of Wight endured many military forays by a series of invaders. Only intensive research could reveal the 'template' for this experience.

What mechanism could cause this 'replay' of past events? Dr McHarg suggested that memories storied in what C. G. Jung called the collective unconscious are responsible. But if this is so, something in the physical setting must trigger the recollection, must 'press the button' that causes the brain to respond with its stored knowledge of the place.

It is just as likely that the physical surroundings themselves store the record of the event, the pattern of activity being printed indelibly on the place by the intense emotion generated by mass activity and a temporary unification of purpose. The subsequent presence in the neighbourhood of a person whose electrical brain patterns happen to 'resonate' in some way with those of the 'record' might result in a translation of the record into audio-visual experiences.

Perhaps in the future observers with correctly trained and 'tuned' mental equipment will be able to pick up the signals given out by large-scale present-day gatherings. For any crowd gathered together with a common purpose generates a high emotional charge (possibly an enhanced electrical potential) – whether they be football crowds or political demonstrators, carnival celebrators or spectators at royal weddings. Perhaps the global events we record today on videotape will in the future be replayed psychically.

Football supporters exult as their team scores a goal. The emotions aroused by the mock battle on the field can be almost as intense as those of a real battle. Will gatherings such as this – a phenomenon of the 20th century – provide material for collective apparitions in the future?

Index